SPIRITS OF THE BORDER
VOLUME II:
THE HISTORY AND MYSTERY OF
FORT BLISS, TEXAS

BY

KEN HUDNALL

WITH

CONNIE WANG

OMEGA PRESS
EL PASO, TEXAS

Figure 1: Brigadier General Howard Bromberg and his wife Glenda Bromberg on the porch of the Pershing House.

Figure 2: Pershing House

SPIRITS OF THE BORDER, VOLUME II

THE HISTORY AND MYSTERY OF FORT BLISS, TEXAS

OMEGA PRESS
An imprint of Omega Communications

For Information Address:

Omega Press
5823 N. Mesa, #823
El Paso, Texas 79912

Or

http://www.kenhudnall.com

FIRST EDITION

ISBN:
ISBN:

Printed in the United States of America

OTHER WORKS BY THE SAME AUTHOR

MANHATTAN CONSPIRACY SERIES

Blood on the Apple
Capital Crimes
Angel of Death
Confrontation

THE OCCULT CONNECTION SERIES

UFOs, Secret Societies and Ancient Gods

WHEN DARKNESS FALLS

SPIRITS OF THE BORDER
(with Connie Wang)

The History and Mystery of El Paso Del Norte

DEDICATION

As always, I must begin by saying that a book such as this cannot possibly be done without help. So it behooves me to thank those who gave of themselves in order to allow me to finish this undertaking.

First and foremost, I must thank Sharon, my wife who has put up with me wanting to wander through strange places and fill the house with bizarre books. Without her, none of what I do would be possible. She is a treasure beyond compare.

Then there is Connie Wang, my co-author, who unselfishly gave of her knowledge and her limited time to insure that this book is the best that it can be.

Glenda Bromberg was a source of information and suggestions that was simply unbelievable. She was always ready to help me find answers. She and BG Bromberg were unfailingly supportive.

It was Colonel (P) Lennox and his family who really got my investigative juices flowing with the fantastic ghost tour that they conducted for myself and a small group of friends. When they offered the Fort Bliss Ghost Tour as a prize in the ADA Gals silent auction, they had no idea what they were unleashing on the unsuspecting United States Army.

Pam Green, the wife of MG Stanley Green gave me the benefit of her knowledge of the history of the post and also took part in the Great Fort Bliss Ghost Tour.

Twister Gerry at the Fort Bliss Museum was a source of encouragement and suggestions that allowed me to avoid many pitfalls that I would otherwise have dove into head first. He opened his records to me without any reservations.

My greatest source of information of course came from Heidi Crabtree. Without knowing it, Heidi Crabtree had led the way with her own book on the events at Fort Bliss. With her research as a starting point, the job was somewhat easier.

8 Spirits of the Border

TABLE OF CONTENTS

CHAPTER ONE
SOME EARLY HISTORY

Fort Bliss, Texas has been a fixture in El Paso for over a hundred and fifty years. There is not a person familiar with the US Military that is not aware of the existence of Fort Bliss, however, only a very few are fortunate enough to know the true history of this historic old post. In these pages, it is hoped that a true picture of what happens when the sun sets on El Paso can be portrayed.

The military post that now bears the name of Fort Bliss is one of the oldest and largest military installations in the continental United States. Though now well established for over a century, it has not always occupied the ground upon which it now sits. In fact, for a time, there was doubt as to whether the post would continue to exist at all. During its existence, this post has been moved several times, captured by enemy troops and then completely abandoned, but somehow, someway, in spite of all of the hardship that fate and location could place in its path this Post has endured all of these changes with remarkable aplomb.

The strategic importance of this area was quickly recognized by the Spanish Conquistadors. El Paso Del Norte[1] occupies is located at the borders of Texas, New Mexico and the Mexican State of Chihuahua. Due to a quirk of

---

[1] The Pass to the North

nature, it was at this location, near what is now the La Hacienda Restaurant, that the mighty Rio Grande was fordable by the Spanish forces with their large wheeled carts[2]. Couple the ease of crossing the river with the existence of one of the few easily accessible passes through the mountains and it is clear why El Paso assumed such importance in the plans of the Spanish Military.

Of course, the exploration of the North American continent was not without its dangers. The Rodriguez-Chamuscado Expedition arrived at El Paso Del Norte on June 5, 1581[3]. This expedition moved from El Paso into New Mexico where one of the first religious settlements was established by the three priests that accompanied the small military force. One priest left to return to Mexico and was killed by Indians and the other two stayed behind after the soldiers left and were also killed.

No discussion of El Paso Del Norte would be complete without a discussion of Don Juan Onate, whose expedition passed through El Paso Del Norte on April 20, 1598[4]. Onate passed through and kept heading northward, eventually reaching Socorro, just south of Albuquerque.

In 1659, Catholic Missionaries settled in what is now Cuidad Juarez and began work on La Mission Nuestra Senora de Guadalupe. It was from this mission that the good Fathers crossed the river to covert the natives and look for gold. The Lost Padre Mine, located somewhere in the Franklin Mountains was worked by the Padres and their followers. The harsh treatment of the natives of Northern New Mexico by their Spanish overlords led to the Pueblo Revolt in 1680. All those of European descent who could, fled to El Paso for safety. The Spanish military forces station inn the El Paso area offered at least some safety from marauding Indians. So intense was this revolt against Spanish authority that it took Spanish forces almost 13 years to restore order and reconquer Santa Fe.

Unfortunately, for the Spanish, the reconquering of Santa Fe did not end their problems with the Indian tribes. It was later found that the Spanish, had in fact, been the impetus for the creation of their greatest foes. The introduction of the horse into North America, while necessary to the exploration and conquest of the rich North American continent also resulted in the creation of the greatest enemy the Spanish had to face. During the Pueblo Revolt, in fleeing death, the Spanish settlers had abandoned many of their valuable horses. Many took to the wilds and it was these horses that were the beginnings of the wild mustang herds that began to appear across the southwest. The American Indians took to the horse with unbelievable swiftness and became some of the finest light cavalry in the world. The Comanches became so proficient at mobile warfare that they drove the fierce Apaches from the southern plains[5].

---

[2] Hudnall, Ken and Connie Wang, Spirits of the Border: The History and Mystery of El Paso Del Norte, Omega Press, 2003.
[3] Metz, Leon C., Desert Army: Fort Bliss on the Texas Border, Mangan Books, 1988
[4] Ibid
[5] Ibid

To deal with this worsening Indian problem, the Spanish Military authorities sent the Marquis de Rubi to improve the frontier defenses[6]. The Marquis urged the creation of a line of fortifications to protect the northern borders of New Spain, which was ordered in the Royal Regulations of 1772[7].

One move made by the Spanish Commander, Colonel Hugo O'Connor, an Irish Mercenary and commander of the northern frontier, was to transfer the presidio of Guajoquilla from southern Chihuahua to San Elizario in 1774. In 1780, the Presidio of San Elizario was moved five miles outside of El Paso.

In 1827, Ponce de Leon a wealthy Paso Del Norte, the original name of Ciudad Juarez, petitioned for land in what is now downtown El Paso. He built a home and several residences for his employees. His holdings became known as Ponce's Rancho and comprised the land now occupied by the Civic Center, the Art Museum, the Camino Real Hotel and some adjacent land.

The small village of Paso Del Norte, on the south side of the Rio Grande, continued to grow and attract settlers. The rule of Spain gave way to the rule by Spanish descended Mexicans. Many Americans were moving into the area that is now Texas, beginning to worry the Mexican authorities, who were continually worried about revolts by the steadily growing Anglo population. Finally, the rumors gave way to reality and Santa Ana, commander of the army and the current ruler of Mexico marched north with a great army to put down the rebellions.

Many Texans were undecided about independence until Santa Ana's forces committed the atrocities at Goliad and Santa Ana himself massacred the defenders of The Alamo. As a result of Santa Ana's own actions, Texas rallied to join Sam Houston. At the Battle of San Jacinto, Santa Ana was defeated and this defeat resulted in Texas winning its independence from Mexico in 1836.

The Treaty of Velasco, signed by Santa Ana as both military commander and President of Mexico, granted Texas independence and established the Rio Grande as the southern border of the newly independent Republic of Texas. This treaty, later repudiated by Santa Ana, transferred Ponce's Ranch and all of the other communities north of the Rio Grande into Texas.

Between the granting of independence by Mexico in 1836 and the beginning of war between the United States and Mexico, the Republic of Texas had an uneasy relationship with Mexico. Though granted everything north of the Rio Grande, including New Mexico and Santa Fe, Mexican forces continued to oppose Texas' attempt to extend its authority over these areas. As an example, the Santa Fe Expedition of 1841 was met and captured near Tucumcari, New Mexico by Mexican forces and the survivors marched to Paso Del Norte and then on to Mexico City.

One of the major problems facing the Texans was the location of the agreed upon borders. Frontiers were hastily drawn in 1848 and even those that

---

[6] Ibid
[7] Ibid

were defined existed in vastly different form than they do now. Even in 1848 there was a great deal of confusion about exactly what border references actually referred to. For example, "Paso Del Norte" originally referred to the gorge along which the Rio Grande flows to pierce the mountain wall, but later became the name of the Spanish settlement now called Ciudad Juarez[8].

Originally, the western border of Texas was not far beyond the line running from Ringgold Barracks at Davis Landing on the Rio Grande, through San Antonio, Austin and Waco. No one knew where the border was located between Texas and New Mexico as it had not yet been established. El Paso at the time was a tiny three building settlement called Franklin on the north bank of the Rio Grande[9]. As a result of the confusion, the military was a little vague in its decision as to the exact location of a military post at Franklin or El Paso as it came to be known.

It is often said that the right man at the right place at the right time can cause tremendous changes. Such was the case in the 1840s, when an influx of entrepreneurs and frontiersmen arrived at the Pass and stimulated steady growth in this formerly backwater area. Frank White opened and operated a trading post at Frontera. Simeon Hart a native New York who had been injured while campaigning in Mexico moved to El Paso Del Norte with his new wife, the daughter of a prosperous Mexican and began to build Harts Mill, where the Hacienda Restaurant now sits beside the Rio Grande. James Magoffin, a former trader, constructed his hacienda, called Magoffinsville, near the intersection of what is now Magoffin and Willow streets[10]. Two miles east of Magoffinsville, Hugh Stephenson, a native of Kentucky, had established his large ranch and also operated a well known trading post near what it now Concordia Cemetery.

The activities of these and other well known names in Texas history resulted in the final establishment of the community of Franklin, named after Benjamin Franklin Coons which later became known as El Paso.

---

[8] Fort Bliss News, *First Post of El Paso Was No Home, Sweet Home*, Page 5, 1948.
[9] Ibid.
[10] Ibid

CHAPTER TWO
UNITED STATES MILITARY PRESENCE

After the conclusion of the war with Mexico, U.S. military authorities recognized the need for a road to connect isolated El Paso with the rest of Texas. So during the winter of 1848, John Ford, a Texas Ranger and Major Robert S. Neighbors, US Indian Agent for Texas opened a direct route from Austin to El Paso. At about the same time, Lieutenant William Whiting of the US Army Engineering Corp and Lieutenant William Smith of the Topographical Engineers surveyed a military road from San Antonio to El Paso. The military road became known as the lower road while the route from Austin became known as the upper road[11]. Both routes were in use by mid-1849 and proved to be a tremendous aid to the 49ers heading for the gold strikes in California.

At the time these roads were beginning to become heavily used by gold seekers heading for California, El Paso left New Mexico to become a permanent part of Texas. In 1850 El Paso County, "the largest county in the largest state in the greatest republic on earth[12]" was formed with San Elizario becoming the first county seat. As originally formed El Paso County entailed 8,450 square miles and reached more than a hundred miles along the Rio Grande.

---

[11] Ibid
[12] Jones, Harriot Howze, El Paso: A Centennial Report. A Project of the El Paso County Historical Society, Superior Printing, Inc. El Paso, Texas 1972

Figure 3: Major Jefferson Van Horne (1802 - 1857)

As has always been the custom in the United States the successful conclusion of a war saw the reduction of the standing army. The Indians of Texas and New Mexico saw this as an opportunity to begin their own war against what they saw as an invasion of their lands. In response to these attacks, Secretary of State Randolph Marcy decided that there needed to be better protection along the border and ordered the construction of a line of forts along the Rio Grande between Santa Fe and El Paso Del Norte. On November 7, 1848, the War Department issued General Order No. 58, ordering the 3rd Infantry Regiment to establish a headquarters in Department No. 9, New Mexico. Thus began the permanent military presence in El Paso.

To carry out General Order No 58, Washington dispatched elements of the 3rd Infantry Regiment, to include the Regimental Staff, Companies A, B, C, E, I and K as well as a howitzer battery from the 2nd Artillery[13]. Major Jefferson Van Horne, a 47 year- old veteran of Indian Campaigns in Florida and the Mexican War, was placed in command. On June 1, 1849, Major Van Horne led his command out of Camp Salado, located near San Antonio, for the long journey to El Paso, arriving in San Elizario on September 1 where they spent several days inspecting the fortifications of the Presidio. Finally they left San Elizario on September 4th, stopping over in Socorro and Ysleta on September 6th and arriving in El Paso on September 8, 1849[14].

As is always the case, no matter how secret, word of the military's plans

Figure 4: Drawing of the Post established at Ponce De Leon/Smith's Ranch, 1849.

to establish a permanent Post in El Paso had spread through the community and the entrepreneurs who had settled in El Paso were not slow to react. Benjamin Franklin Coons, a local merchant saw the financial opportunity a military presence would bring and immediately began to look for a suitable spot to place the post. The presence of the First Dragoons at Ponce's Hacienda led him to believe that this would be the best location for a larger more permanent post and accordingly, he purchased the land that had been the Ponce de Leon Hacienda for the enormous sum of $18,000.00. Upon the arrival of Major Van Horne and the 3rd Infantry, Coons leased the main buildings and an additional six acre tract, including the land where the Plaza Theatre, the Art Museum the Chamber of Commerce and the Civic Center now sit, to the army for the large sum of $4,200.00 per year.

---

[13] Antone, Evan Haywood, A Tribute to Major Jefferson Van Horne, Founder of Fort Bliss, Ft. Bliss, Museum, Ft. Bliss, Texas. 1998
[14] Ibid

From his letters, it appears that Major Van Horne was less than enamored with the new quarters and rather than give the new Garrison a proper name, he called it "The Post Opposite Paso del Norte". In those days, of course, Paso Del Norte referred to what is now Ciudad Juarez. The post was also considered to be in New Mexico, since the current boundaries between Texas and New Mexico had not yet been established.

THE POST OPPOSITE EL PASO

When Major Van Horne arrived at what is now El Paso, he found a growing community on the south side of the Rio Grande and several small communities on the north side. There was James Magoffin's Magoffinsville; Benjamin Franklin Coons holdings called Franklin; Hugh Stephenson's property was called Concordia; Simeon Hart's hacienda and mill at Molino and Frank White's Frontera. The overall area was designated as Franklin, named after the holdings of Benjamin Franklin Coons, the major power broker in the area. It was not until 1852 that the Postmaster General of the United States designated the American held areas across from the Mexican Town of Paso Del Norte as El Paso[15].

Once arriving in El Paso, Major Van Horne was faced with making the decision as to how best to protect the area. He chose to divide his command, quartering four companies at Ponce's Ranch and detaching two other companies, Companies I and K, under the command of Major William S. Henry, to man the Presidio at San Elizario. Van Horne had serious planned to quarter his entire command at the Presidio due to its superb fortifications, but the uproar of local merchants caused him to make the final decision that he did to divide his command and man both areas[16].

According to established history, the military establishment that became Fort Bliss, established in February 1848, was located at a point on what is now Magoffin Avenue, near the Concordia Cemetery and was known as Camp Concordia[17]. This location may have been the beginning of what has become known as Ft. Bliss, but it was certainly not the first United States military presence in the El Paso area.

Even earlier, there was a military presence here with the arrival of Colonel A. B. Doniphan in 1846, the man responsible for extending the sovereignty of the United States into this District[18]. Colonel Doniphan, a

---

[15] Ibid
[16] Ibid
[17] Crimmins, Colonel Martin L., _Local History_
[18] Graves, Betty, El Paso High School, Del Norte Council NO. 2592, El Paso, Texas, 1931 Essay Contest, _Old Fort Bliss_, Western American, October 3, 1931, 6th Honorable Mention.

Kentucky lawyer, commanded the 1st Regiment of Mounted Missouri Volunteers. With the advent of the Mexican War, Colonel Doniphan led his men south along the Chihuahua Trail toward Mexico. At what is now Vado, New Mexico his force was opposed by over a thousand mounted Mexican soldiers. These dedicated Lancers were determined not to allow Doniphan and his men to approach El Paso Del Norte, now Ciudad Juarez. These Mexican Lancers were dedicated and brave, but, unfortunately they were poorly led and no match for the rifle fire of the American forces.

In the ensuing battle, the Mexican cavalry raised the flag of "No Quarter" and charged the American forces intending to run them down and sweep them from the battlefield, but the horsemen were cut to pieces by deadly accurate rifle fire. In disarray, having lost many men dead or wounded, the Mexicans withdrew from the field and Doniphan moved into El Paso with his brigade of Missouri Mounted Volunteers and remained here until late in 1847 when the military pulled out of El Paso completely.

In 1848, the Mexican Government signed the Treaty of Guadalupe Hidalgo and the United States assumed sole responsibility for all lands north of the established Mexican/US Border. Though the United States had assumed responsibility for the health and welfare of all of those living in what had been part of Mexico, the Regular Army had its hands full dealing with an ever increasing Indian problem. There were simply not enough troops to cover every area that needed to be garrisoned.

Prior to the arrival of Major Van Horne and the 3rd Infantry, in September 1849, on February 11, 1848, a detachment of the First Dragoons, under the command of Major Benjamin Beall, made camp on the Franklin Coons Ranch, where the present day Camino Real Hotel now stands. The detachment had been chasing Indians throughout the mountains above El Paso and established a permanent base camp in a few abandoned adobe shacks on the Coons Ranch[19].

The purpose of this detachment of the First Dragoons establishing their small post was to protect the residents of the area from the depredations of the Indians who were continually raiding the local ranches. Additionally, this small post also served as a hospitable inn and a bank for weary travelers[20].

With the arrival of the 3rd Infantry, the Coons property began to achieve a much more prominent role in local affairs as Major Van Horne also chose to quarter his forces on the Coons property. From the arrival of this military force until its transfer to Fort Fillmore in New Mexico on April 15, 1851, the 3rd faithfully discharged its duty of protecting the citizens of the area.

However, it is a fact of life that all good things must end and so it was that the War Department ordered that the "post opposite Paso Del Norte be

---

[19] El Paso Herald Post, _Old Ft. Bliss Noted School for Generals_, May 28, 1936.
[20] El Paso Times, _Fort Bliss Has Grown From Adobe Shacks Into One of Great Assets Here_, October 25, 1931.

abandoned." A small detachment remained at the Presidio in San Elizario until September 5th, when they too departed for Fort Fillmore.

So ended the first military establishment at El Paso.

CHAPTER THREE
FORT BLISS

Even though the 3rd Infantry was assigned to Fort Fillmore and this post was just outside of Mesilla, New Mexico, El Paso residents still felt unprotected from attacks from marauding Indians. There were continual requests from the citizens of El Pas as well as lobbying in Washington to have troops once again assigned to El Paso. Finally, growing tried of the continual requests, and becoming aware of the importance of El Paso as a post, on March 8, 1954, the War Department issued General Order No. 4, signed by Secretary of War Jefferson Davis. In this General Order, it was specified that the military post near El Paso would be re-established and would hereafter be known as Fort Bliss. The naming of the post Fort Bliss was to honor Colonel William Wallace Smith Bliss (1815-1853), son in law of former President Zachary Taylor and Inspector of the Army until his death in 1853 of yellow fever.

To staff the new post, the War Department detailed Companies B, E, I and K of the 8th Infantry, who were stationed at Fort Chadbourne, Texas. Lieutenant Colonel Edmund B. Alexander was designated commander of this new post at El Paso and he assumed command on January 11, 1854[21]. The returning military forces opted not to reactivate the abandoned "post opposite Paso Del Norte" at Coons, now Smith's ranch. Instead facilities were leased from James Magoffin between what is now Willow and Walnut Street in the Bassett addition[22]. The new Post in Magoffinsville served the military well until the beginning of the Civil War in 1861.

---

[21] Metz, Leon C., Desert Army: Fort Bliss on the Texas Border, Mangan Books, El Paso. 1988.
[22] El Paso Times, *Fort Bliss Occupied Numerous Sites Before Finding Home on Present Magnificent Domain*, September 28, 1921.

Figure 5: One of the few known views of the Post at Magoffinsville, the first official Fort Bliss.

THE CIVIL WAR YEARS

The coming War Between the States severely divided the country and the citizens of El Paso as well. The Mills Brothers were ardent Unionists while Simeon Hart and James Magoffin were stanch Confederates. This led to a great deal of debate and ill will between the various factions that formed in the town.

Just as the country was split, there was also a split within the United States Army as well, with many officers being from the South and they, naturally, favored the Southern Cause. On December 8, 1860, Fort Bliss was transferred to the Department of Texas from the strongly Union Military Department of New Mexico. The commander of the Department of Texas was General David Emmanuel Twiggs, one of the Army's three full Brigadier Generals. He was a southern sympathizer, but nevertheless, he asked Washington for instructions as to how to deal with the crisis. When no instructions were forthcoming, he surrendered all U.S. Military property in Texas to state authorities before the Civil War even started[23]. Of all of the officers stationed at Fort Bliss, only Colonel Isaac Reeve, 8th US Infantry and Fort Bliss commander, and Lieutenant Lazelle remained loyal to the Union.

On March 31, 1861, Colonel Reeve ordered the flag of the United States lowered at the military post in El Paso for the last time and surrendered the fort to Joseph Magoffin, Confederate Commissioner[24]. Colonel Reeve marched his command out of the post toward the east, picked up others companies of the 8th

---

[23] Metz, Leon C., <u>Desert Army: Fort Bliss on the Texas Border</u>, Mangan Books, El Paso. 1988.

[24] Fort Bliss News<u>, "Confederate Stars and Bars Replaced "Old Glory" At Bliss For Seventeen Months During Civil War</u>", Page 3, November 5, 1948.

Infantry Regiment at Fort Quitman and Fort Davis enroute to the gulf coast and transportation out of the south. Near San Antonio, Colonel Reeve was forced to surrender his command to Confederate Colonel Earl Van Horne. Colonel Van Horne had under his command 1,400 Confederates under Colonel H. E. McCullough, 1st Regiment, Texas Mounted Rifles[25]. Colonel Reeve and his men of the three garrisons who had remained loyal to the United States spent the remainder of the war in confinement.

On July 1, 1861, about 300 Texans of the 2nd Regiment of Texas Mounted Rifles under the command of Colonel John R. Baylor occupied Fort Bliss. Colonel Baylor, apparently a man who thought big, declared himself Governor of the Territory of Arizona and continued in his self appointed position until the arrival in December of Brigadier Henry Sibley and his Brigade of 3,700 men who was sent by Jefferson Davis to establish the Army of New Mexico and to conduct a campaign to conquer New Mexico and California for the South. The Confederate government had a serious need for the gold that conquering California would add to its coffers and felt that General Sibley could easily defeat the few Union forces between his Army and the Pacific coast.

The plan was sound, but General Sibley was the wrong man in the wrong place. He knew little of the southwest and liked the bottle too much to be the Commander needed for such a daring scheme.

The Confederate invasion of New Mexico began in February, 1862, with great fanfare and high hopes. As Sibley's force moved west, it fought several battles with Unions forces under the command of General Canby, the most important of which was the Battle of Valverde, a battle that both sides claimed to have won. Sibley still had a powerful force at his command, but by late April 1862, a combination of the inhospitable land, lack of water and Union forces had destroyed Sibley's ability to continue the campaign and ended his dreams of conquest. The Confederates, now numbering about 2,000, returned in defeat to El Paso and reoccupied Fort Bliss in early May of 1862. Upon learning that the reinforced Union force was moving to engage him and fearing a further defeat by the advancing Union forces, Sibley ordered what was left of his command to retreat to the east, after destroying anything useable by the Union forces. By the end of July 1862, the last Confederate forces had left El Paso, opening the way for its occupation by Colonel James Carleton and his California Column.

In August 1862, Company C of the California Column was encamped at Hart's Mill. The California Column remained in El Paso until October 15, 1865 until the arrival of the 5th Infantry Regiment. This Regiment assumed garrison duties for El Paso and the Border Area.

---

[25] Ibid.

CAMP CONCORDIA

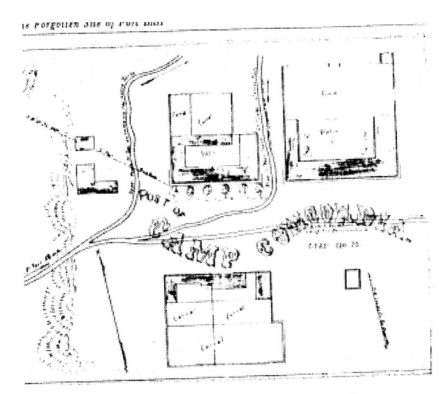

Figure 6: Diagram of Camp Concordia

The 5th Regiment settled into garrison life and returned to the post at Magoffinsville, unfortunately the facility was in a shambles as a result of years of neglect, as well as vandalism by the locals. During the years the post was abandoned, some of the buildings had been carried away for scrap lumber for other construction and others had fallen into ruins. Reoccupying the post was not easily accomplished as advanced units found that in addition to the damage caused by neglect and vandalism, Mexican squatters had turned some of the remaining structures into their homes. Removing the squatters from the only homes they had caused a great deal of ill will among the Mexican community.

The impetus for a move by the Army to new quarters materialized in May of 1867 when the Rio Grande flooded, washing away storerooms and portions of the officers' quarters. Rather than undertake the tremendously difficult job of rebuilding the ruined post, the military leased property from the Hugh Stephenson estate and work was begun on a new facility to be called Camp Concordia. In March of 1868, Camp Concordia was completed and the military officially moved out of the post at Magoffinsville. On March 11, 1869, Camp Concordia was renamed Fort Bliss.

However, there were tough economic times ahead for the Country, the Military and for El Paso. In January 1877, to save money, the Government permanently abolished Fort Bliss, transferring all troops to other locations. This was a short sighted decision that proved to be very bloody for El Paso, for there was a major problem brewing regarding the ownership of Salt flats below Guadalupe Peak. With no military presence to keep things under control, tempers quickly got out of hand.

For many years, Mexicans had obtained salt from these beds at no cost, ignoring the attempts of El Paso politicians to collect fees from those that took the salt. As always, those in office looked for ways to get more money out of the civilian population and charging for salt seemed like a good way to get a little extra into the pot, so to speak. This difference of opinion resulted in a large number of political killings, most of which were ignored, but when attorney Charles Howard killed his partner Judge Luis Cardis, who had sympathized with the Mexicans, this was the straw that broke the proverbial camel's back. The people of San Elizario rose up and a full-scale insurrection ensued. So enraged were the people of San Elizario over the murder of Judge Cardis, that when a company of Texas Rangers arrived to try and restore order, they were overwhelmed and forced to surrender to a San Elizario mob[26]. As a matter of interest, in its entire history, this is the only time that a company of Rangers has been forced to surrender.

To deal with the mushrooming problem, Colonel Edward Hatch, commander of the Military District of New Mexico rushed to San Elizario with elements of the 9th Cavalry, and Companies A, G and I of the 15th Infantry. The arrival of these veteran military units put an abrupt end to the Salt War.

In his after action report, Colonel Hatch recommended re-establishing a military presence in the El Paso area to ensure that there was not a similar reoccurrence of violence. However, Colonel Hatch's efforts were not needed for Congress had already authorized re-establishing a military post at El Paso and on New Years day 1878, Fort Bliss once again was an active military post.

GARRISON TOWN

Company L of the 9th Cavalry and Company C of the 15th Infantry were the first units to be assigned to the new post and upon arriving in El Paso, they attempted to reoccupy Camp Concordia, but found it to be in total ruins. After some futile efforts to repair the old facilities, with little success, the military rented space in downtown El Paso near San Jacinto Plaza. The new quarters were built on the corner of Mills and Oregon streets where the Federal Building stands

---

[26] Ibid

today[27]. Military headquarters was located at the corner of El Paso and San Antonio Streets. For the next two years, the troops remained in what was called Garrison Town, living in abandoned buildings that had been hastily converted into barracks and drilling on the public streets.

However, progress was coming rapidly to El Paso. The railroad had arrived in El Paso and Garrison Town was right in the middle of the business district. Though the business community had moved heaven and earth to convince Congress to re-establish a military presence in El Paso, greed was outweighing patriotism. So much business was coming into El Paso that the every available building was needed as businesses expanded rapidly. The buildings occupied by the military were only rented from the owners and the owners could get a bigger return using the buildings for business purposes. Therefore, the Army had to move.

Finally, giving in to the pressure from business leaders in El Paso, the military decided that it needed a more permanent home and better quarters for the troops. In 1879, General Order No 27 authorized the construction of a new post near El Paso. So a search began that lasted several months for a new permanent location. Finally it was decided to obtain 135 acres beside Hart's Mill. Simeon Hart was paid $100.00 for this land upon which the new post would be constructed.

Thus, in December 1880, the military moved into the new facility. General Sherman favored retaining the name Ft. Bliss and Secretary of War Alexander Ramsey made it official on July 8, 1879.

---

[27] Graves, Betty, El Paso High School, Del Norte Council NO. 2592, El Paso, Texas, 1931 Essay Contest, *Old Fort Bliss*, Western American, October 3, 1931, 6th Honorable Mention.

OLD FORT BLISS AT HART'S MILL

Figure 7: Old picture of the Post at Hart's Mill

The facility that is now called Old Fort Bliss was established in 1881. Buildings were erected just north of Hart's Mill on the smelter road and attempts were made to give the new post every amenity, or at least more than were available for the troops in Garrison Town[28]. One unusual aspect to this new Post was that the estimate of the cost of construction by the contractor was so outrageously high that it was decided to let the troops build the Post[29]. Unfortunately, the construction work was continually interrupted by the troops being called away to combat Indian raiding parties, so work proceeded slowly[30].

There was no question that the new post at Hart's Mill was a major improvement over Garrison Town, but it still had some problems. The Rio Grande, uncontrolled by the last Elephant Butte Damn, would flood periodically and continually threatened to wash away the post. The standing pools of water were breeding grounds for mosquitoes and since the drinking and wash water came from the Rio Grande, most of the troops suffered from dysentery. The location was considered very unhealthy by military medical authorities.

Additionally, growth of Fort Bliss was considered impossible due to the Rio Grande that bordered on the Post and the problems caused by the hilly terrain

---

[28] El Paso Times, *Fort Bliss Occupied Numerous Sites Before Finding Home on Present Magnificent Domain*, September 28, 1921.
[29] Fort Bliss News, *Century-Long History of Old Fort Bliss Told in Pictures*, Page 12, November 5, 1948.
[30] Ibid.

surrounding the post. Everyone recognized that an inability to grow a military post limited its usefulness and could result in the post being eliminated. Additionally, when the railroads arrived in 1881, the Santa Fe Railroad, with the permission of Congress, laid tracks through the middle of the parade ground. The Southern Pacific Railroad passed just outside the eastern perimeter of the Post.

A final consideration was that tactically, Fort Bliss was in a very vulnerable situation. If an attacking enemy gained control of the high ground across the Rio Grande, Fort Bliss would become untenable, as it could not be easily defended. Attempts to assault the high ground from the post would be suicidal.

Figure 8: "La Chiquita Cafe" located at 1932 Paisano Drive was once the old guard house of Old Fort Bliss

Then finally, there were political issues again raising their ugly heads inn Washington. The Army and the Railroad had worked out an arrangement whereby the Railroads would transport the soldiers and the soldiers would protect the Railroads. Plans were therefore made to consolidate the many small forts across the west into larger regional posts adjacent to rail lines. Thus in the case of New Mexico and Texas, General Sheridan had decided that while Fort Bliss was the more strategically located, it could not be expanded and thus Fort Selden outside Las Cruces should be expanded and Fort Bliss closed.

Luckily, General Sherman, then the Army Chief of Staff, decided that Fort Bliss was too important to close. He felt that Fort Bliss could become a Regimental sized Infantry Post supported by small Cavalry Posts at strategic locations along the border, but he also knew that the Post would have to be moved to a more practical location where it could grow.

On March 1, 1890, President Benjamin Harrison signed a $150,000.00 appropriation for a new Fort Bliss to be built within 10 miles of El Paso. The new post was to consist of approximately 600 acres, an amount of felt to be suitable in size to house a twelve-company garrison. However, upon closer reading, it turned out that the bill signed by President Harrison only allotted money for the building of the Post, not for the purchase of the land. Therefore, if El Paso wanted to keep Fort Bliss it would have to give the Army the land upon which to build the new post. The citizens of El Paso rose to the challenge and raised the money necessary to purchase, and donate to the Army, the necessary 600 acres on the mesa at a site known as "Lanoria" or the well.

However, after the donation, the Army then said it needed 1,000 acres, not six hundred. Obligingly, the citizens of El Paso raised the money to obtain the additional four hundred acres and it too was donated to the new post. Then the Army was concerned that there was no close source of water to meet the needs of the proposed facility. So El Paso citizens paid for the drilling of a well near the location chosen for the main Post that luckily struck a spring of crystal clear water. Now, everyone believed, the new Fort Bliss could begin to rise from the mesa as the government had promised for so long. But, unfortunately, the requests from the Army were not ended as of yet.

Captain George Ruhlen of the Quartermaster Corps arrived from Washington to inspect the post. In spite of the major effort undertaken by the citizens of El Paso to give the military exactly what it wanted, he determined that Fort Bliss needed the southwest edge of the Mesa to keep undesirable elements from establishing businesses adjacent to the post. This land had not been donated as part of the original 1,000 acres. So with no thought of the hardships his demand would cause, he wanted the citizens of El Paso to once again donate land, fifty acres this time, to the military. Somewhat less enthusiastically than before, the citizens of El Paso raised the money to purchase this additional fifty acres and donated it to the new post. This land was used for the construction of Officers Row.

All looked promising for a bright future, but the Army had one more request. It wanted an additional two hundred acres donated to the new post. The citizens of El Paso felt that it was being shaken down by the military. Either give up more land or no post was the way it was put to the good citizens according to the news accounts of the day. There was a strong feeling that this was going far beyond anything the government had a right to expect, but in an attempt to keep relations cordial, the citizens, with some difficulty, raised the money to purchase and donate the additional 200 acres. So Fort Bliss began with 1,266 acres donated by the citizens of El Paso.

In February 1893, initial construction was completed on the new Fort Bliss. On October 27, 1893, the Regimental headquarters, the Band and Companies A, C, D and H of the 18th Infantry arrived from Fort Clark, Texas to become Fort Bliss's first occupants. Captain William H. McLaughlin became the first commander of the new post.

The structures that comprised at what is now called Old Fort Bliss located at Hart's Mill were sold at auction to the highest bidder and the military cemetery located where the Public Library now sits was donated to the city. Fort Bliss now had a permanent home.

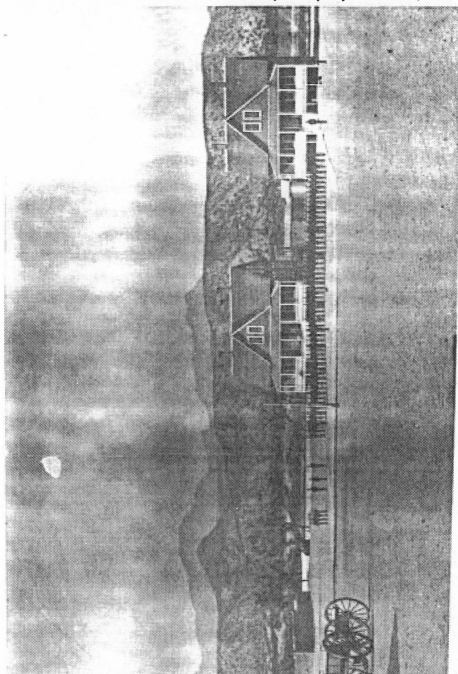

Figure 9: Fort Bliss at Hart's Mill[31], (1880-1881)

---

[31] Photo from author's collection.

CHAPTER FOUR
ECHOES OF THE PAST

In discussing the history of Fort Bliss, or any other location, it is easy to forget that this location also contained the history of a lot of men and women who lived and loved in these buildings that we take for granted. Some of them leave behind what I can only call echoes of their lives for those with the ability to see these echoes. Such is certainly the case with a military post that has such a long history and that has seen the amount of death and violence that has played such a part of Fort Bliss' history.

There has been a great deal of talk about the hauntings and other spooky events in some of the buildings located at Ft. Bliss, but just as humans leave things behind when they move, it also seems that as Fort Bliss has moved it has also left things behind. This chapter will deal with hauntings that I think are associated with Fort Bliss at locations that it has previously occupied. This will, naturally, result in some cross over with Volume I of Spirits of the Border[32], but I think that to tell the complete story of the hauntings of Fort Bliss, that all locations need to be discussed and it will certainly give some more detailed information to some of the stories of hauntings that have made the rounds lately.

I have given a very sketchy history of Fort Bliss, now settle back and read about the mystery that surrounds this historic old post.

---

[32] Hudnall, Ken and Connie Wang, Spirits of the Border: The History and Mystery of El Paso Del Norte, Omega Press, El Paso, Texas. 2003

THE HAUNTINGS OF THE
PONCE DE LEON/COONS/SMITH RANCH

As outlined in the previous chapters, the original military encampment was on the land originally owned by Ponce de Leon which was purchased by Benjamin Franklin Coons to become known as the Coons Ranch and after his financial ruin, resold to become known as Smith's Ranch. Not A great deal is known about the Smith after whom the property was named, it is known that "Billy" Smith occupied the proper in 1853[33]. The military only occupied this property for a few years, on two different occasions, but it was enough to leave its mark permanently upon the land.

As outlined earlier, the Coons Ranch area occupied by the 3rd Infantry occupied the ground upon which today sits the Camino Real Hotel, the El Paso Convention Center, the El Paso Art Museum, the El Paso Chamber of Commerce and the Plaza Theater. As discussed in *Spirits of the Border: The History and Mystery of El Paso Del Norte*[34] each of these locations is haunted and most of them are haunted by more than one spirit.

To the buildings mentioned above, you can also add the El Paso City Hall, adjacent to the Convention Center as well as the Mills Building, near the Plaza Theater and the Main Public Library, which occupies the land that was the first military cemetery. The Plaza Hotel, across the street from the Camino Real Hotel was the first Hilton to bear the Hilton name and also has its share of ghosts. Why are there so many spirits within such a small area of land? Some of the ghosts at the Library appear to be military related, such as the Confederate soldier seen reading a magazine, but who vanishes if approached and the 'Captain' who wanted his chair to sit in one specific location and who, if someone moved his chair, would move it back.

It is said that prior to Ponce De Leon building his hacienda in this location that another grandee built a beautiful hacienda where the Plaza Theater now stands. He was a jealous man and his wife was very young and very beautiful. He built their home so far from Paso Del Norte so that he could keep her from seeing other men. She spent her days delighting in her beautiful rose garden. One day the husband returned home and, believing that his wife had received visitors while he had been gone, flew into a jealous rage, believing that she was seeing another man behind his back. He became so enraged at the thought that she had seen another man in his house, that he strangled his young wife and buried her body in her rose garden. Overcome with remorse, he burned down his beautiful hacienda and rode away, but she still tends her beloved

---

[33] Fort Bliss News, *First Post of El Paso Was No Home, Sweet Home*, Page 4, November 5, 1948.
[34] Hudnall, Ken and Connie Wang, <u>Spirits of the Border: The History and Mystery of El Paso Del Norte</u>, Omega Press, El Paso, Texas. 2003.

flowers, having been often seen watering the plastic flowers that decorates the top one of the artificial, inaccessible balconies in the Plaza Theater.

So it would seem that some of those who lived at Ponce's Ranch during their time in the 3rd Infantry still mount their guard and still carry out their duties. Though this is nowhere near today's Ft. Bliss, this was the location of the first U. S. military presence in El Paso and it is only proper that it be included in a book about the mysteries of Ft. Bliss.

POST AT MAGOFFINSVILLE

At this time, I do not have any information regarding hauntings in this area. However, research is ongoing and anything found will be included in another volume regarding El Paso.

CAMP CONCORDIA

As if to make up for the lack of activity at Magoffinsville, what had been known as Camp Concordia has a great deal of unusual, unexplainable activity.

What once was a bustling Army Post is now a place of the dead, with victims of violent death lying side by side with innocents cut down by illness or accident. El Paso has an unusually violent history. In fact, the violence and lack of respect for law prevalent in El Paso during the 1880s was enough to earn the town the sobriquet "Hell Paso."[35] There is actually no way to know how many might have met a violent end in El Paso if not for the presence of the Army at Fort Bliss.

El Paso's 'Saloon Row' was a testing ground for would be fast guns from all over the west that were itching to gain a reputation. The wild and wooly atmosphere in El Paso attracted killers from almost every state. Many outlaws whose exploits rivaled those of Billy the Kid made El Paso their home away from home, but Billy the Kid himself never set foot in the Border Town. One example

---

[35] Fort Bliss News, *"Hell Paso" Too Rough Even for Bill The Kid*, Page 3, November 5, 1948.

of the exploits of some of the gunmen who made El Paso their home was John Wesley Hardin who used his fast gun reputation every chance he had.

On one occasion, he went into a Saloon, slapped a hundred dollar bill down on the bar and declared that he was now half owner of the establishment[36]. On another evening, he raked in a large poker hand and declared himself the winner, even though he did not hold the winning hand[37]. In neither instance did anyone challenge him, fearing certain death from his deadly weapons. Ironically, it was his reputation as a cold blooded killer that actually led to his own death when Constable John Sellman thought it best to shoot first and ask questions later when he came upon Hardin in the Acme Saloon. Hardin was famous for shooting 'over the shoulder' with deadly accuracy using the many mirrors that were found in most saloons. When Sellman came into the Acme Saloon and spied Hardin at the bar watching him in the mirror, Sellman drew and shot Hardin in the back, killing him. Hardin now lies beneath the rocky soil of Concordia Cemetery, where once soldiers drilled under the hot Texas sun.

Some of the unexplained events at Concordia Cemetery were discussed in Spirits of the Border: The History and Mystery of El Paso Del Norte[38], but suffice it to say that a number of people who have had occasion to walk past the silent cemetery after dark have reported hearing the sounds of the hoof beats of unseen horses as well as the sounds of conversations being carried on by unseen speakers. Rhythmic footsteps of unseen people heard on some nights could well be troops drilling, unaware that their periods of military service ended long ago.

Based on available evidence there are many spirits from the Camp Concordia days who still make themselves known to the land of the living as they carry out their duties. Drilling, riding, and doing all of the things that a soldier would be called upon to do, the sounds of these activities can be heard at various times. Adding to the spirits from the Camp Concordia days are those of the occupants of the original post cemetery, located where the Main Public Library now sits. There eternal rest was disrupted when some of the bodies were moved when the City decided to use the property for building. However, it is estimated that in many cases the workers assigned to move the bodies, the town drunks, merely moved the headstones.

As reported in *Spirits of the Border: The History and Mystery of El Paso Del Norte*[39], patrons of the L & J Café, adjacent to Concordia Cemetery have heard the sounds of hoof beats as well as chains being drug through the gravel. Fort Bliss may have moved to another location, but the troops formerly stationed there, or a part of the troops, stayed behind, still holding guard mount until the day that they are relieved by the highest authority of all.

---

[36] Ibis

[37] Ibid

[38] Hudnall, Ken and Connie Wang, Spirits of the Border: The History and Mystery of El Paso Del Norte, Omega Press, El Paso, Texas. 2003

[39] Ibid

GARRISON TOWN

When it became clear that the buildings of Camp Concordia could not be salvaged for military use, the military presence in El Paso moved once again, this time to rented buildings in downtown El Paso around the San Jacinto Square area, very near its original location at Ponce's Ranch.

This entire area, that once encompassed this incarnation of Fort Bliss, is well known to contain many haunted buildings. In almost every case, when discussions of spirits that have been seen in these buildings are compiled, the mention is made of the spirits of soldiers. Once again, it seems that as Fort Bliss moved from location to location, it left something of itself behind.

HARTS MILL
OLD FORT BLISS

Figure 10: The Hacienda Restaurant formerly the home of Simeon Hart.

After Garrison Town, Fort Bliss moved to 135 acres beside Harts Mill. A new post was built more in keeping with military necessity, to include a series of quarters for the officers of the command. During the period of time the post functioned in this location, a large number of troops passed though and those permanently stationed there saw a lot of action in the continuing war with the Indians.

In February 1848, General Sterling Price, not realizing that the Mexican War was over, crossed the Rio Grande at La Hacienda and occupied present day Juarez. He then moved south and occupied Chihuahua City. One of his soldiers was Simeon Hart, a native of New York who was wounded in the fighting in southern Chihuahua. Hart was cared for in the home of a wealthy Mexican miller whose beautiful daughter acted as his nurse. In December 1849, Simeon Hart married Jesusita Siqueiros, his former nurse. Hart was 41 and Jesusita was 17 at the time of their marriage. The couple came to El Paso and built their homestead and a flour mill along the designs of the one her father has constructed in Mexico[40].

---

[40] Metz, Leon C., Some Facts About the Hacienda. Date Unknown.

By March 21, 1850, the Hart homestead, called La Hacienda, was flourishing and Simeon Hart's Mill was functioning at full capacity. Hart had contracts to furnish flour to both of the fort Bliss Posts[41]. Th Butterfield Overland Stage stopped at what had become known as Hart's Mill on its way from Socorro. By 1850, there was also a damn and irrigation system stemming from the area around La Hacienda. Though the old mill has long faded into history, Simeon Hart left an indelible imprint on the land. The hacienda upon which he lavished so much love is now the La Hacienda Restaurant. All that is left of the sprawling old military post are some of the officers' quarters that sit adjacent to the restaurant – and some restless spirits that have been seen by many over the years.

The La Hacienda, of course has a number of fairly well publicized spirits as outlined in Spirits of the Border: The History and Mystery of El Paso Del Norte[42]. However, the adjacent buildings, the former military officers' quarters that represent all that is left of the old post, also have their share of spirits that have never left. These historic old structures have been renovated and are rented out as apartments. There have been some interesting old stories told about things that have happened here.

Figure 11: These were formerly the quarters built for the officers at the post at Hart's Mill. These few structures are all that is left of the old post.

---

[41] Fort Bliss as well as the post at San Elizario.
[42] Ibid

I have had more than one individual tell me that ghostly figures have been seen moving through the quarters at night.

CHAPTER FIVE
NEW FORT BLISS

Congress had authorized the funds to begin construction of what was being called "New Fort Bliss" in 1890. The designation of "New Fort Bliss" was temporarily added to distinguish the new post from "Old Fort Bliss" located at Hart's Mill.

The importance of Fort Bliss had become well apparent to military planners as a result of a wide variety of disturbances and crisis situation that had arisen along the border in the previous generation. There had been the Cortina War from 1859 to 1860, the Kickapoo and Mescalero Fighting from 1873 to 1877, Apache fighting from 1860 to 1886 and numerous bandit and Indian raids of short duration[43]. In addition to these events there was also the Sheridan Expedition immediately after the Civil War[44], sent by President Andrew Johnson.

Because of the continuing need to keep troops along the border with Mexico, it was decided that small, 2 to 4 company military posts should be established. A post at El Paso was considered of prime strategic importance due to the city's location at almost the center of the Southwest Border as well as the large railroad complex in El Paso. There was also a continually expanding trade

---

[43] Historic American Building Survey No. TX-3339, 7th Cavalry Buildings, U.S. Army Air Defense Artillery Center and Fort Bliss, City of El Paso, El Paso County, Texas.
[44] Ibid

with Mexico, mining operations in the area, mail service, banking and utilities, a reasonable climate and a most co-operative local population. For these and other reasons, it was decided to expand Fort Bliss.

Figure 12: New Fort Bliss, 1895[45]

The final design of the 'New' Fort Bliss was largely due to the work of the Constructing Quartermaster Officer, Captain George Ruhlen[46] who was assisted in this endeavor by F. A. Gartner, architect and civil engineer and Edward H. Offley, chief clerk. Ruhlen's design took into account the future expansion of the post even though the plans provided for a traditional four company Infantry Post. The initial plans called for the Post to have a commanding officer, a surgeon, four captains, eight lieutenants, as well as two enlisted men's barracks. After some wrangling and numerous modifications, the final plans for the new post included fourteen officers' quarters, four enlisted men's barracks, a mess hall, a hospital, a pump house, a commissary and quartermaster warehouse and several other support buildings.

During this first period of building at the new post, the Classical Revival style dominated with Greek Revival and Queen Anne influences being evident in building trim and wood porch ornamental detail. Construction was in brick, with the use of ornamental terra cotta gable end trim and red sandstone bush hammered and ashlar sills, lintels and water tables[47]. The gable roofs had tin shingles and the officers' quarters and enlisted men's barracks had wood porches. The officers' porches were screened while those on the enlisted men's barracks were open. The buildings in the Quartermaster group were primarily constructed of gray rubble and ashlar limestone with bush hammered and ashlar red sandstone trim and with gable roofs and tin shingles.

---

[45] This photo came from a story in the Fort Bliss News dated November 5, 1948.
[46] Ibid
[47] Ibid

Figure 13: Captain George Ruhlen[48] (1847-1933)

When the new post opened in 1894, four companies of the 18th Infantry arrived at Fort Bliss form Fort Clark, Texas to become the first troops to occupy the buildings and these companies provided the basic garrison for the Post during the 1890s. With the Indian Wars at an end, the 1890s was a time of peace at the new post.

---

[48] Photo from author's collection.

In the fall of 1895, Troop A of the 5th Cavalry was ordered to Fort Bliss and stables were constructed for the horses. This was the first time in the almost fifty years that Fort Bliss had been in El Paso that a cavalry unit was permanently stationed here. This lone cavalry troop was the beginning of a trend that would see Fort Bliss become the major horse cavalry post on the Southwest border[49].

The Spanish-American War had an immediate impact on Fort Bliss. The four companies of the 18th Infantry stationed at the Post as well as Troop A of the 5th Cavalry were sent first to New Orleans and then to wartime service in the Philippines and Puerto Rico. In fact, throughout the period of the Spanish-American War (1898-1902), Fort Bliss had only a skeletal garrison. Indeed in the absence of regular Army forces, Texas State Troops performed most of the garrison duties. From July 1898 until July 1899, Fort Bliss was garrison by volunteer troops including the Texas Volunteer Cavalry and later by a company of the 3rd Texas Volunteer Infantry. Until relieved by regular Army units once again, these volunteer troops guarded the volatile border with Mexico.

The years between the Spanish-American War and World War I passed quietly at Fort Bliss; it remained a small post and was considered a frontier assignment. However, looming on the horizon was the brewing revolution in Mexico and the events that would catapult Fort Bliss into its role as a major horse cavalry post.

However, with its new importance still some years in the future, the new Post had fallen into considerable disrepair. Building exteriors had fallen victim to the harsh weather of the Southwest had the interiors reflected the lack of continued maintenance. Lieutenant Colonel H. H. Adams of the 18th Infantry command the post in 1902 and he reported that only 9 of the 39 buildings on the post were in good condition. He also reported that the temporary pump house was worthless and in terrible condition; the hospital steward's quarters and the stables were in need of extensive repairs; and the remaining twenty-seven buildings were also seriously in need of extensive repairs[50].

Though the Army moves slowly, the right ears had gotten wind of Fort Bliss' deteriorating condition. In 1905 and 1906 building exteriors were repaired and building interiors were refurbished. Additionally, the post also received badly needed landscaping and road improvements. Due to its strategic location, Fort Bliss had some very highly placed supporters.

For example, in 1903 Brigadier General Frederick D. Grant, son of the former President and Civil War General, and commander of the Department of Texas pointed out the importance of railroad communications to the military and the serious need for a post in El Paso, the site of one of the largest railroad complexes in the Southwest. BG Grant said:

"One of the first considerations which must enter into the maintenance of military stations along the Mexican frontier is the necessity for absolute

---

[49] Ibid
[50] Ibid

command or control in time of war or other great public danger of any and all of the great international railroad lines which have so extensively grown in the pat twenty years. For this reason El Paso must always be regarded as a strategic point, on account of being the most important railroad junction, next to Fort Worth and Houston, in the Southwestern United States[51]. "

The Mexican Revolution, which has long been called one of the greatest upheavals in Latin American History, began in 1910 and ended in 1920. It was during this tumultuous ten-year period that the importance of Fort Bliss was finally proven once and for all.

Wars and revolutions bring out the worst in man and also, if a man is smart, can make his a millionaire. The Revolution in Mexico was no exception. The fighting in Mexico spilled over the border into the United States on more than one occasion and the continued border violations, shootings, arms smuggling, bandit raids and other problems magnified by the chaos in Mexico resulted in an increased American military presence along the International Border. For the very first time since being established, Fort Bliss played a major role in local, regional and national history[52].

There was also a certain unreality to the Mexican Revolution due to the continued presence of Pancho Villa and his men in and around El Paso during the early part of the Revolution. Indeed, there are many stories about Pancho Villa attending parties and luncheons at the Paso Del Norte Hotel and he even stayed at the Pershing House on Fort Bliss as the guest of none other than General "Black Jack" Pershing himself.

However, Villa's fondness for El Paso and his friendship with General Pershing soon came to an end thanks to Villa's changing political fortunes and American political expediency. Villa reacted to what he viewed as betrayal, according to established history, by attacking Columbus, New Mexico setting the stage for what has been called the most famous event of the Mexican Revolution, the Pershing Expedition of 1916-1917 where General Pershing was sent to chase his former friend Pancho Villa through the wilds of Mexico[53].

---

[51] Ibid

[52] Ibid

[53] There is another side to this story as well. While stationed at Fort Benning, Georgia, I had occasion to spend some time in the historical records in the Infantry School Library's 'cage'. According to what I read among the old papers stored there, Pancho Villa may have been paid the sum of $250,000.00 in gold to stage the attack on Mexico to give US forces the opportunity to train under actual field conditions for the upcoming war in Europe in which US Military leaders felt the US would eventually become involved.

Supporting the idea that the Pershing Expedition was a contrived realistic training exercise paid for with tax payer dollars, are a number of stories from the descendants of men that went into Mexico with Pershing who have reported that on many evenings Villa would come down from the hills to play cards and socialize with his old friend, General Pershing. Then with the dawn, Villa would return to his own forces and the chase would commence once again.

Military historian Clarence C. Clendenen wrote that it is no exaggeration to say that the Punitive Expedition of 1916 gives the continuity between the American Soldier of the Civil War and the Indian Wars and the American Soldier of World War II, Korea and Vietnam. It is not too much to say that the Mexican Punitive Expedition of 1916 and 1917 was a training school for the greater war (World War I) that was soon to follow.

There is no question that the Pershing Expedition, whether a true pursuit as history claims, or a contrived training exercise as many old soldiers and their descendants around El Paso claim, was the first major test of the United States Army in the twentieth century. This was the first time that airplanes were used in actual combat conditions and the use of motorized transportation systems and untried logistical systems were tested.

It was also during this tumultuous period that Fort Bliss took on new responsibilities. It became a central base for border patrols and of course it was the main supply base for the Pershing Expedition. However, in addition to these fair well known functions, it also tried to control the flow of weapons into Mexico as well as serving as a reception center for the flood of Mexican refugees, wounded civilians and soldiers as well as prisoners all of whom flocked north seeking to escape the fighting[54]. During this period, Fort Bliss was also the host to a massive National Guard mobilization and build up of other troops that poured into Fort Bliss. To accommodate this ever-growing force, a ring of auxiliary camps was built around the post and around the El Paso area.

It was also during this period of unrest along the border that a large number of officers came to Fort Bliss whose names would ring down through history. General Pershing was of course already well known, but very few know that Lieutenant George S. Patton, Jr. was at Fort Bliss and went into Mexico with Pershing's force[55]. First Lieutenant James L. Collins, brother to J. Lawton (Lightening Joe) Collins of World War II fame served as Pershing's aide de camp in 1915. Colonel Peyton March, Army Chief of Staff in 1918, was stationed at Fort Bliss in 1916 with the 8th Field Artillery. Finally, Lieutenant Colonel Selah R. H. "Tommy" Tompkins of the 7th Cavalry accompanied

---

[54] Ibid

[55] How Lieutenant (and future General) George S. Patton came to join General Pershing's force is quite a story. This little publicized story about George Patton was related to me by Glenda Bromberg and her husband, Brigadier General Howard Bromberg, one warm later summer afternoon. It seems that Patton was indeed stationed at Fort Bliss with the 8th Cavalry Regiment, but he was not selected to join Pershing's force. However, no one counted on Patton's determination and the lengths he would go to in order to accompany General Pershing. Lieutenant Patton actually camped out on the porch of Pershing House, and slept in the hallway at the bottom of the stairs so that every day when General Pershing would leave for his office, the first thing he would see would be the young Lieutenant. Pershing already had an aide de camp and no place for another new Lieutenant, but Patton's persistence finally wore Pershing down and he finally allowed Patton to join his Expedition.

Pershing and he commanded the 7th Cavalry when this famed unit took part in the Juarez Race Track Skirmish of 1919[56].

On September 21, 1921, the unit with the longest association of any unit with Fort Bliss, the First Cavalry Division was formally established at Fort Bliss as a regular Army Division. The first commander of the new division was Major General Robert L. Howze. The division consisted of a Division Headquarters unit, a First Cavalry Brigade, consisting of the 1st and 5th Cavalry Regiments; a Second Cavalry Brigade, composed of the 7th and 8th Cavalry Regiments; the 82nd Field Artillery Battalion (Horse); the 8th Mounted Engineers; the 1st medical Squadron; the 1st Signal Troop; the Division Trains. All of the Division was located at Fort Bliss except for the 1st Cavalry located at Camp Marfa and the 5th Cavalry located at Fort Clark, Texas[57].

When the First Cavalry Division left Fort Bliss to take part in the war against the Japanese in the Pacific Theater, this was the end of the mounted cavalry as part of the United States Army. Fort Bliss as the home of the Cavalry was to have a new mission. From World War I through World War II, Korea, Vietnam, and the two wars in the Middle East, the mission of what was called "New" Fort Bliss has changed with the times. Now it is the home of the Air Defense Artillery.

However, old soldiers do not like change and apparently some old soldiers have not wanted to leave what they looked at as their home. "New" Fort Bliss has a large number of ghosts that seem determined to continue to stand their duty stations. In the next chapters, some of these gone but not forgotten specters will be discussed. However, for each one mentioned in these pages, I am sure that there are several that have been overlooked.

Over the course of its long history, Fort Bliss has evolved from a small infantry outpost on the far frontier to a major cavalry post to an antiaircraft training school and a guided missile testing center. The Fort Bliss of today is the home of the Army's Air Defense School and the U.S. Army Sergeants Major Academy and consists of over 300 buildings built during several different building periods and constructed according to several different architectural styles. What follows is an overview of the buildings constructed during each period.

The initial construction period was from 1891 through 1899 and during this time period 27 buildings were constructed[58]. These were the first buildings constructed on the new fort Bliss and as a result they represent a mix of residential, Administrative and support facilities. Family housing is located on the west side of the parade ground, with barracks, administration and support buildings being located on the east side.

---

[56] Ibid
[57] Ibid
[58] National Register of Historic Places Registration Form for the Fort Bliss Main Post Historic District, 2nd Edition, November 2000.

Buildings Constructed During the Initial Period[59] (1891-1899)

Building. Number	Date of Construction	Original Use
8	1893	Hospital
9	1893	Isolation Ward
13	1893	Enlisted Barracks
19	1893	Bathhouse
21	1893	Mess Hall, Library, HQ
111	1893	Double Barracks
128	1893	Pump house & Boiler
219	1893	Captain's Quarters
220	1893	Lieutenant's Quarters
221	1893	Captain's Quarters
222	1893	Lieutenant's Quarters
223	1893	Lieutenant's Quarters
224	1894	Captain's Quarters
227	1893	Lieutenant's Quarters
229	1893	Lieutenant's Quarters
230	1893	Captain's Quarters
231	1893	Lieutenant's Quarters
232	1893	Lieutenant's Quarters
233	1893	Captain's Quarters
234	1893	Lieutenant's Quarters
235	1893	Captain's Quarters
241	1893	Guardhouse
2009	1895	Wagon & Wheelwright Shop
2011	1893	Quartermaster Stables
2019	1895	Forage Shed
2021	1893	Quartermaster Storehouse
2022	1897	Storehouse

As the Post expanded, more construction was necessary and the Army entered into an interim period of construction from 1900 through 1912 in order for the Post to undertake its mission as a border installation[60]. It was during this period that the use of the Army's standardized construction plans, such as Building 228, the Commanding Officer's Quarters, built according to the Quartermaster General's Plan Number 243.

---

[59] Ibid
[60] Ibid

Building Constructed During the Interim Period[61] (1900-1912)

Building Number	Date of Construction	Original Use
1	1904	Base Hospital
51	1904	Post Library
53	1909	Post Exchange, Canteen-Bowling
129	1910	Elevated Water tower
228	1910	Commanding Officer's Quarters
275	1912	Arms Storage Magazine
2010	1908	Horseshoeing Shop

Beginning in 1913, work was undertaken to convert Fort Bliss from an Infantry Post to a major cavalry installation. The buildings added to Fort Bliss during this construction program, are referred to as the First Expansion Period Group. The impetus for this building spurt was to support Fort Bliss' role as a cavalry post designed to prevent arms smuggling across the Mexican Border and to discourage and respond to any hostile acts against the United States.

Standardized plans utilized during this period of construction included Enlisted Men's Barracks CQM-341, Mess Hall and Kitchen CQM-342 as well as plan # CQM-371, Lieutenant's Quarters CQM-338 and Captain's Quarters CQM-337. Architectural, many of the buildings in the group display features of the Colonial Revival, Prairie style bungalow, and Craftsman style bungalow[62].

Buildings Constructed During the First Expansion Period Group[63] (1913-1917)

Building Number	Date of Construction	Original Use
4	1914	Hospital Isolation Ward
5	1915	Ambulance Garage
11	1915	Enlisted Men's Barracks
12	1915	Enlisted Men's Barracks
15	1915	Mess Hall & Kitchen
55	1916	Telephone Exchange & Barracks
112	1915	Enlisted Men's Barracks
113	1915	Enlisted Men's Barracks

---

[61] Ibid
[62] Ibid
[63] Ibid

Buildings Constructed During the First Expansion Period Group[64]
(1913-1917)
Continued

Building Number	Date of Construction	Original Use
114	1915	Enlisted Men's Barracks
115	1915	Enlisted Men's Barracks
116	1915	Enlisted Men's Barracks
117	1915	Enlisted Men's Barracks
118	1915	Enlisted Men's Barracks
122·	1915	Mess Hall & Kitchen
123	1915	Mess Hall & Kitchen
125	1915	Mess Hall & Kitchen
127	1915	Mess Hall & Kitchen
201	1914	Lieutenant's Quarters
202	1914	Lieutenant's Quarters
203	1914	Lieutenant's Quarters
204	1914	Lieutenant's Quarters
205	1914	Lieutenant's Quarters
206	1914	Lieutenant's Quarters
207	1914	Captain's Quarters
208	1914	Captain's Quarters
209	1914	Captain's Quarters
210	1914	Captain's Quarters
211	1914	Captain's Quarters
212	1914	Captain's Quarters
213	1914	Captain's Quarters
214	1914	Captain's Quarters
215	1914	Captain's Quarters
216	1914	Captain's Quarters
217	1914	Captain's Quarters
218	1914	Captain's Quarters
225	1914	Captain's Quarters
226	1914	Captain's Quarters
236	1914	Captain's Quarters
237	1914	Captain's Quarters
238	1914	Captain's Quarters
239	1914	Captain's Quarters
240	1914	Captain's Quarters
242	1917	Post Electrical Substation
888	1916	Ammunition Warehouse
889	1916	Ammunition Warehouse

---

[64] Ibid

Buildings Constructed During the First Expansion Period Group[65]
(1913-1917)
Continued

Building Number	Date of Construction	Original Use
890	1916	Ammunition Warehouse
1310	1917	Post Pumping Plant
1441	1915	Post Bakery
2014	1917	Veterinary
2020	1917	Administration Building

The next building period was in connection with the assignment of the Seventh Cavalry to fort Bliss. The nine buildings built at fort Bliss during 1919 are associated with the original 7th Cavalry Cantonment area. The construction of this cantonment was part of the early efforts of the War Department to create a cavalry division along the U.S.-Mexican Border. These particular buildings generally do not display any specific significant architectural style.

Buildings Constructed During the 7th Cavalry Construction Period Group[66]
(1919)

Building Number	Date of Construction	Original Use
440	1919	Mess Hall
442	1919	Mess Hall
443	1919	Mess Hall
444	1919	Mess Hall
448	1919	Enlisted Men's Barracks
449	1919	Enlisted Men's Barracks
450	1919	Enlisted Men's Barracks
451	1919	Enlisted Men's Barracks
452	1919	Enlisted Men's Barracks

The next building period that took place on Fort Bliss is referred to as the Second Expansion Period and refers to those buildings built during 1918-1926. Historically, these buildings were built in response to the adding of twenty-four Mexican Border Zone Warehouses and several other support structures to Fort Bliss. This construction was part of a larger effort on the part of the U.S. Army to more efficiently manage its supply operations and to make Fort Bliss the national

---

[65] Ibid
[66] Ibid

premier Mexican border post. These buildings do not display any specific significant architectural style.

Buildings Constructed During the Second Expansion Period[67] (1918-1926)

Building Number	Date of Construction	Original Use
54	1919	Fire Station
250	1919	Officer's Open Mess
273	1921	Recruiting Office
315	1924	7th Cavalry Service Club
1101	1921	Ordinance Office and Warehouse
1102	1921	Warehouse
1103	1921	Warehouse
1104	1921	Warehouse
1105	1921	Warehouse
1106	1921	Warehouse
1107	1921	Warehouse
1108	1921	Warehouse
1109	1921	Warehouse
1110	1921	Warehouse
1111	1921	Warehouse
1112	1921	Warehouse
1113	1921	Warehouse
1114	1921	Warehouse
1115	1921	Warehouse
1116	1921	Warehouse
1117	1921	Warehouse
1118	1921	Warehouse
1119	1921	Warehouse
1120	1921	Warehouse
1121	1921	Warehouse
1122	1921	Warehouse
1123	1921	Warehouse
1124	1921	Warehouse
1125	1921	Warehouse
1126	1921	Warehouse
1127	1921	Warehouse
1128	1921	Warehouse
1334	1921	Motor Vehicle Repair Garage
1336	1921	Riding Hall
1361	1919	Quartermaster Granary

---

[67] Ibid

Buildings Constructed During the Second Expansion Period[68] (1918-1926)
Continued

Building Number	Date of Construction	Original Use
1372	1918 (1941)	Scale house and Scale ways
1456	1920	Tailor Shop
1480	1923	Medical Dispensary
2004	1926	Clothing Store
2032	1920	Loading Dock

The next construction era at Fort Bliss is referred to as the Depression Era and runs from 1927 to 1939[69]. Historically, these new buildings are associated with the major building program that added many new officers' and non-commissioned officers' quarters, barracks, stables, garages and other support structures to the installation. This building program at Fort Bliss was part of a larger nationwide Army building program that stretched from 1927 to 1939. This building program played an important role in implementing government sponsored Depression era relief programs.

Buildings Constructed During the Depression Era Expansion Period[70]
(1927-1939)

Building Number	Date of Construction	Original Use
243	1939	Bachelors Officers' Quarters
244	1936	Officers' Garage
246	1936	Garage
247	1936	Garage
248	1937	Post Officers' Club Servant's Quarters
251	1934	Girl Scout House
265	1936	Garage
266	1936	Garage
267	1936	Garage
268	1936	Garage
269	1936	Garage
270	1936	Garage
271	1936	Garage
272	1936	Garage
301	1934	Officers' Quarters
302	1934	Commanding Officer's Quarters

---

[68] Ibid
[69] Ibid
[70] Ibid

Buildings Constructed During the Depression Era Expansion Period[71]
(1927-1939)
Continued

Building Number	Date of Construction	Original Use
303	1934	Officer's Quarters
304	1934	Officer's Quarters
305	1934	Servant's Quarters
306	1934	Officer's Garage
311	1938	War Department Theater
317	1930	NCO Quarters
318	1930	NCO Quarters
319	1930	NCO Quarters
320	1930	NCO Quarters
321	1930	NCO Quarters
322	1930	NCO Quarters
323	1930	NCO Quarters
324	1930	NCO Quarters
325	1930	NCO Quarters
326	1930	NCO Quarters
327	1930	NCO Quarters
328	1930	NCO Quarters
329	1930	NCO Quarters
330	1930	NCO Quarters
331	1930	NCO Quarters
332	1930	NCO Quarters
333	1930	NCO Quarters
334	1930	NCO Quarters
335	1930	NCO Quarters
336	1930	NCO Quarters
337	1930	NCO Quarters
338	1930	NCO Quarters
339	1930	NCO Quarters
340	1930	NCO Quarters
341	1930	NCO Quarters
342	1930	NCO Quarters
343	1930	NCO Quarters
344	1939	NCO Quarters
345	1939	NCO Quarters
346	1939	NCO Quarters
347	1939	NCO Quarters
348	1939	NCO Quarters

[71] Ibid

Buildings Constructed During the Depression Era Expansion Period[72]
(1927-1939)
Continued

Building Number	Date of Construction	Original Use
349	1934	NCO Quarters
350	1934	NCO Quarters
351	1934	NCO Quarters
353	1934	NCO Quarters
354	1934	NCO Quarters
355	1934	NCO Quarters
356	1934	NCO Quarters
357	1934	NCO Quarters
400	1934	Officer's Quarters
401	1934	Officer's Quarters
402	1934	Officer's Quarters
403	1934	Officer's Quarters
404	1934	Officer's Quarters
405	1934	Officer's Garage
406	1934	Officer's Quarters
407	1934	Officer's Quarters
408	1934	Officer's Quarters
409	1934	Officer's Quarters
410	1934	Officer's Quarters
411	1934	Officer's Quarters
412	1934	Officer's Quarters
413	1934	Officer's Quarters
414	1934	Officer's Garage
415	1934	Officer's Garage
425	1934	Officer's Garage
426	1934	Officer's Quarters
427	1934	Officer's Quarters
428	1934	Officer's Quarters
429	1934	Officer's Quarters
500	1934	Enlisted Men's Barracks
503	1934	Enlisted Men's Barracks
504	1934	Enlisted Men's Barracks
512	1934	Enlisted Men's Barracks
515	1934	Enlisted Men's Barracks
516	1934	Enlisted Men's Barracks
522	1934	Officer's Quarters
523	1934	Officer's Quarters

[72] Ibid

Buildings Constructed During the Depression Era Expansion Period[73]
(1927-1939)
Continued

Building Number	Date of Construction	Original Use
524	1934	Officer's Garage
525	1934	Officer's Quarters
526	1934	Officer's Quarters
527	1934	Officer's Quarters
528	1934	Officer's Quarters
529	1934	Officer's Quarters
530	1934	Officer's Quarters
531	1934	Officer's Quarters
532	1934	Officer's Garage
533	1934	Officer's Garage
534	1934	Officer's Garage
535	1934	Officer's Garage
536	1934	Officer's Quarters
537	1934	Officer's Quarters
538	1934	Officer's Quarters
539	1934	Officer's Quarters
540	1934	Officer's Quarters
541	1934	Officer's Quarters
542	1934	Officer's Quarters
543	1934	Officer's Quarters
544	1934	Officer's Quarters
611	1934	Blacksmith and Saddle Shop
612	1934	Blacksmith and Saddle Shop
613	1934	Blacksmith and Saddle Shop
614	1934	Cavalry Stables
616	1934	Cavalry Stables
618	1934	Cavalry Stables
620	1934	Cavalry Stables
622	1939	Cavalry Stables
624	1939	Cavalry Stables
627 ·	1934	Stable Guard Quarters
628	1934	Stable Guard Quarters
629	1939	Stable Guard Quarters
631	1939	Stable Guard Quarters
632	1939	Stable Guard Quarters
633	1939	Stable Guard Quarters
635	1939	Cavalry Stables

---

[73] Ibid

Buildings Constructed During the Depression Era Expansion Period[74]
(1927-1939)
Continued

Building Number	Date of Construction	Original Use
639	1939	Cavalry Stables
641	1939	Cavalry Stables
643	1939	Cavalry Stables
645	1939	Cavalry Stables
649	1939	Blacksmith and Saddle Shop
650	1939	Blacksmith and Saddle Shop
651	1939	Blacksmith and Saddle Shop
730	1936	Garage
762	1939	Organization Garage
769	1939	NCO Quarters
801	1939	NCO Quarters
1400	1933	NCO Quarters
1401	1933	NCO Quarters
1402	1933	NCO Quarters
1403	1933	NCO Quarters
1404	1933	NCO Quarters
1405	1933	NCO Quarters
1406	1933	NCO Quarters
1407	1934	NCO Quarters
1408	1934	NCO Quarters
1409	1934	NCO Quarters
1410	1939	NCO Quarters
1411	1939	NCO Quarters
1412	1939	NCO Quarters
1413	1939	NCO Quarters
1442	1930	NCO Quarters
1443	1930	NCO Quarters
1444	1930	NCO Quarters
1445	1930	NCO Quarters
1446	1930	NCO Quarters
1447	1930	NCO Quarters
1448	1930	NCO Quarters
1449	1930	NCO Quarters
1450	1930	NCO Quarters
1451	1930	NCO Quarters
1452	1930	NCO Quarters
1453	1930	NCO Quarters

[74] Ibid

Buildings Constructed During the Depression Era Expansion Period[75]
(1927-1939)
Continued

Building Number	Date of Construction	Original Use
1454	1930	NCO Quarters
1457	1930	NCO Quarters
1458	1930	NCO Quarters
1459	1930	NCO Quarters
1460	1930	NCO Quarters
1461	1930	NCO Quarters
1462	1930	NCO Quarters
1463	1930	NCO Quarters
1464	1930	NCO Quarters
1465	1930	NCO Quarters
1466	1930	NCO Quarters
1467	1930	NCO Quarters
1468	1930	NCO Quarters
1469	1930	NCO Quarters
1470	1930	NCO Quarters
1471	1930	NCO Quarters
1472	1930	NCO Quarters
1473	1930	NCO Quarters
1474	1930	NCO Quarters
1475	1930	NCO Quarters
1476	1939	NCO Quarters
1477	1939	NCO Quarters
1478	1939	NCO Quarters
1479	1939	NCO Quarters
1481	1930	NCO Quarters
1482	1930	NCO Quarters
1483	1930	NCO Quarters
1484	1930	NCO Quarters
1485	1930	NCO Quarters
1486	1930	NCO Quarters
1487	1930	NCO Quarters
1488	1930	NCO Quarters

The next major period of expansion at Fort Bliss was during the World War II era, 1940 – 1045, though this time the expansion was in terms of land. By the end of the War, the land controlled by Fort Bliss included the 5,000 acres post reservation, 52,000 acres of adjoining land to the east and northeast, the

[75] Ibid

3,272 acre Castner Target Range and the 46,000 acre Dona Ana Target Range in New Mexico. In addition to this land, Fort Bliss leased 350,000 acres of land in New Mexico for use as an antiaircraft range and had trespass rights on another 200,000 acres in New Mexico.

Although little permanent construction was undertaken at Fort Bliss during this time period, the post did gain many standardized wooden temporary-type structures. Between 1941 and 1943, numerous mess halls, barracks, administration buildings, motor shops, recreational buildings, fire stations, latrines, storehouses, theaters, service clubs and other structures were built across the post.

Also included in this flurry of construction were numerous wards and hospital buildings associated with the Fort Bliss Station Hospital (later known as the William Beaumont Hospital Annex), located in the then northeast corner of the Installation.

The next identifiable period of construction associated with Fort Bliss took place during what is called the Post World War II period, designated as those years between 1946 and 1950. Historically, these buildings are associated with the further development of Fort Bliss during the period when the installation was completing it transformation from a cavalry post into the Army's major air defense center following World War II.

The rapid growth of the air defense sector necessitated more housing for fort Bliss. It was also during this period of time that the people of El Paso donated a group of five (5) reconstructed adobe buildings from the original Fort Bliss in honor of that Fort's centennial. The Fort Bliss Replica Museum has been part of the post for nearly fifty years.

Buildings Constructed During the Post World War II Period[76]
(1946-1950)

Building Number	Date of Construction	Original Use
545	1948	Officer's Quarters
546	1948	Officer's Quarters
547	1948	Officer's Quarters
548	1948	Officer's Quarters
549	1948	Officer's Quarters
550	1948	Officer's Quarters
551	1948	Officer's Quarters
552	1948	Officer's Quarters
553	1948	Officer's Quarters
554	1948	Officer's Quarters
565	1948	Officer's Quarters
5051	1948	Museum Building

[76] Ibid

Buildings Constructed During the Post World War II Period[77]
(1946-1950)

Building Number	Date of Construction	Original Use
5052	1948	Museum Building
5053	1948	Museum Building
5053A	1948	Museum Building
5054	1948	Museum Building

The report from which I took this information was designed to discuss those buildings of historical significance that would be placed on the National Register of Historic Places. However, there are other facilities located on post that, while not of historic significance, certainly are of importance to the post. These buildings are listed below and are called non-contributing resources in the report.

Other Buildings on Fort Bliss[78]

Building Number	Date of Construction	Original Use
2	1954	Hinman Hall/Administration
28	1976	Pump house
45	1949	Red Cross - Temporary
46	1941	Red Cross - Temporary
48	1941	Gen. Purpose Admin - Temporary
49	1941	Gen. Purpose Admin - Temporary
50	1941	Gen/ Purpose Admin - Temporary
100	1987	Entrance Directory
101	1987	Waiting Shelter
253	1957	Toilet/Shower
254	1957	Swimming Pool
263	1922	Tennis Court
259	No Date	Tennis Court
313	1949	Flagpole
446	1960	Ball Court
454	1970	Toilet/Shower
455	1964	Water Treatment
505	1955	Gen. Purpose Administration
615	1972	General Purpose
619	1957	Storage
623	1957	Storage
644	1958	Storage

---

[77] Ibid
[78] Ibid

Other Buildings on Fort Bliss[79]
Continued

Building Number	Date of Construction	Original Use
897	1941	Ordinance Repair Shop
898	1920	Ordinance Paint Shop
1170	1932	Turbine Pump House
1177	1941	Warehouse
1178	1941	Warehouse
1179	1941	Warehouse
1180	1941	Warehouse
1181	1941	Warehouse
1235	1928	Latrine
1270	1941	Warehouse
1271	1941	Warehouse
1272	1941	Warehouse
1273	1941	Warehouse
1274	1941	Warehouse
1275	1941	Warehouse
1276	1941	Warehouse
1277	1941	Warehouse
1278	1941	Warehouse
1279	1941	Warehouse
1281	1941	Cold Storage
1301	1941	Exchange/Service Outlet - Temp
1310	1956	Snack Bar
1319	1959	Water Treatment
1326	1966	Fuel/POL Building
1328	1941	Gen. Purpose Maintenance - Temp
1330	1991	Wash Building
1332	1941	Gen. Purpose Administration - Temp
1438	1956	Family Housing
1439	1956	Family Housing
1440	1956	Family Housing
1489	1956	Family Housing
1490	1956	Family Housing
1491	1956	Family Housing
1492	1956	Family Housing
1493	1956	Family Housing
1494	1956	Family Housing
1495	1956	Family Housing
1496	1956	Family Housing

[79] Ibid

Other Buildings on Fort Bliss[80]
Continued

Building Number	Date of Construction	Original Use
1497	1957	Family Housing
1542	1920	Gymnasium
1780	1941	Sewage Disposal Pump
2065	1940	Outdoor Swimming Pool
2528	1941	General Purpose Warehouse
2529	1941	Motor Repair Shop
2535	1941	Flammable Material Storehouse
2637	1943	General Storehouse
2647	1941	Swimming Pool
2650	1940	Motor Repair Shop
2651	1940	Administration
4899	1941	Water Tank

Certainly not all of these buildings contain spirits of those who have gone before, but, based on the many stories that have come from Fort Bliss over the years some of them are certainly haunted. What follows are some of the more common stories.

---

[80] Ibid

CHAPTER SIX
FORT BLISS REPLICA MUSEUM

There are some cases where the location of a haunting is so out of the ordinary that very idea of a haunting is so bizarre that it stretches the imagination. Such is the case with this unusual story of a haunting of the Fort Bliss Replica Museum[81] and its original office located across the street in Building 660. Believe it or not, according to an article by Flo Coulehan[82], the Replica Museum does have a full time spirit of its very own.

When this story came to her attention, Ms. Coulehan was researching a story on ghosts for a local magazine called Paso Del Norte and had gone to see Margaret Blanco, the then director of the Fort Bliss Replica Museum. While seated at Ms. Blanco's desk, Ms. Coulehan had her first experience with the unseen.

As Ms. Coulehan sat at her borrowed desk, she began to feel a wind around her similar to a desert dust devil and a chill swirled upward toward her shoulders. This unexpected wind surprised Ms. Coulehan as the windows were shut tightly and the door to the outside was closed. Since there was really no reason for the sudden coldness, Ms. Coulehan was moved to comment on the draft she was feeling, which brought a surprising reaction from Ms. Blanco.

"It's him!" exclaimed the museum director, rushing over to push up her sleeves and show Ms. Coulehan the goose bumps on her arm. The wind suddenly

---

[81] Buildings 5051, 5052. 5053, 5053A and 5054.

[82] Coulehan, Flo, *Post Plays Host To Ghost*, El Paso De Norte, June 1983.

stopped and Ms. Blanco pulled her sleeve back down and began to relate the story of the Ghost of the Replica Museum.

According to Ms. Blanco, a sudden cold draft was the way in which the resident spirit normally announced his presence. She also added that in addition to a sudden temperature drop, the hair on the arms of anyone present and the hair on the nape of their necks stand up as if there is an electrical charge in the air.

Ms. Blanco said that she thinks the unseen presence is a nice spirit who comes to protect someone or something in the museum. Besides, she added, what self-respecting museum does not have its' own ghost?

Margaret Blanco first became aware of the presence of this ghostly presence in 1974 when she became director of the Fort Bliss Replica Museum. She was quoted in the article as saying that doors would open and close without any explanation and footsteps could be heard crossing empty rooms. She would also see movement out of the corner of her eye, but when she would look in the director of the movement, there would be nothing there.

Figure 14: Fort Bliss Replica Museum[83]

The spirits seems to try to interact with Ms. Blanco and her staff during the day, making appearances in areas other than the office. She said that recently, some painting had been done in one of the galleries and a museum worker turned on a fan in the gallery to blow out the paint fumes. The worker then went to perform some work inn the large room adjacent to the museum's chapel. As he worked, he suddenly realized that the fan had stopped working. Returning to the freshly painted gallery, the worker checked to make sure that the fan was plugged in and that the outlet was still working. He could find nothing wrong. Suddenly, the fan resumed working with no explanation.

Ms. Blanco felt that the ghost's appearance had something to do with the green table in the museum's conference room that was believed to have been

---

[83] This photo came from a story in the Fort Bliss News, dated November 5, 1948.

used by General "Black Jack" Pershing when he was commander of Fort Bliss. Unfortunately, she remarked that they were unable to prove the history of the table, so it was relegated to the conference room where the staff used it for doing paperwork. This conference was one of the spirit's favorite spots.

According to Charles Duncan, the museum's historical adviser at the time of the article had another theory. He felt that the ghost was that of a dead Japanese soldier guarding the Samurai Sword taken from his corpse in World War II. The ceremonial sword was displayed for some time before it had been removed from the public view and placed in storage. However, Bob Edwards, a museum worker mentioned in the article, complained that, even though the sword was in a storage area, every time he went near the display the sword would fall on him as if the spirit of the former owner was angry.

As an aside, I might make mention that some of the Samurai sword taken by soldiers as war souvenirs from dead Japanese were in fact many centuries old. The method of making weapons as sharp as these Samurai Swords has been lost in the mists of time. Some of these swords were very ornately decorated, and could be considered as true works of art. These cherished finely honed implements of dead were passed down through the generations, carried by the oldest male of each generation.

When commissioned as officers for service during World War II, these skilled warriors, steeped in tradition, had their prized swords drafted as well. The ornate decoration was removed and the blades were converted to a military appearance. So it is not impossible to think that the spirits of those who cherished and honored these one of a kind blades might seek to protect them from what they consider as dishonor, being put on display in a foreign land by a conquering army that does not understand the true meaning of such a rare weapon.

There are, naturally, others who believe that the ghost is present due to another item in the museum's care. There is, or was at the time of the article, an antique gentleman's dresser in the museum office that was believed to have belonged to Francis Scott Key, the composer of "The National Anthem". The true of the dresser, like what may be Pershing's conference table, cannot be proven. So until it can be, the dresser is relegated to the museum office rather than displayed for all of the world to see.

The major problem with assigning a reason for the haunting is that few people have ever seen this particular ghost. The Army has a rule, a regulation, or a procedure for almost everything, but not one for determining the provenance of a ghost. However, there was one individual who claimed to have seen the elusive spirit that haunts the Replica Museum.

Specialist 4th class, Silvester Brown was the assistant to the museum technician at the time of the article by Flo Coulehan. According to Specialist Brown, on a clear February morning in 1983, as he approached the facility, he noticed a man in a blue uniform or suit leaning against a tree just in front of the office, apparently attempting to see through the office door. SP4 Brown thought, at first, that his eyes were playing tricks on him because as he got closer, the blue clothed figure got dimmer and dimmer until he vanished completely. He never saw anyone walk or run away form that tree.

Sp4 Brown described the figure he had seen as about six feet tall, weighing over 180 pounds. When he reached the tree where the figure had been standing, he noticed that some bark was missing form the tree. However, according to the article, this experience did change his attitude regarding ghosts somewhat.

One interesting note that is pointed out in the article is that the night before Specialist Brown saw the ghost outside the museum, three civilians and a dog had spent the night inside the museum office in an attempt to get a picture of the ghost. Perhaps what Brown saw was the ghost attempting to get a look at the civilians without allowing himself to be photographed.

There are no known human grave sites on the museum property, but there are four tombstones that can be seen. One marker was erected for an old cavalry horse, named Garry Owen; one was erected for a dog named Major Smokey; a third erected for a mare named Lady and the fourth erected for another horse named Buddy[84]. These graves were unearthed during a building project at the post ad moved to the museum grounds in 1959.

According to Margaret Blanco they are sure the museum is haunted as too many visitors have stopped the moment they enter the office or the museum itself, saying that they feel a presence. These rumors have actually brought more visitors to the museum. Of course, this spirit or spirits are not alone as there have been stories of ghostly sightings at the Moulin Rouge Dinner, Theater, in houses in Officers' Row and at the post cemetery.

No one has ever been able to explain why the Fort Bliss Replica Museum is haunted as there is nothing about this facility that is particularly remarkable. I will point out that the five adobe buildings that comprise the Fort Bliss Replica Museum were donated from the location of the original Fort. Perhaps the spirit that is haunting the museum came with the buildings. The museum office was described as a nondescript wooden building built in 1941 that was used as a processing center and then as a branch bank before becoming the office for the Replica Museum. The reason for the haunting is perhaps a question best answered by the resident ghost and he does not seem inclined to talk.

---

[84] Coulehan, Flo, *Post Plays Host To Ghost*, El Paso De Norte, June 1983

Figure 15: Was this the spirit seen at the Fort Bliss Replica Museum[85]?

---

[85] This photograph was part of the article and is apparently a recreation of the spirit seen by the witness.

CHAPTER SEVEN
BUILDING 1

Figure 16: The front entrance to Building 1. The doors pictured here are said to open and close by themselves.

The building designated as Building 1 is located on Pershing Road, across from Post Headquarters and the Air Defense Artillery School (Building 2). Originally, this building was designated as Building 93 and it was the second hospital to be built on Fort Bliss, replacing Building 8[86] that will be discussed in grater detail later. Building 1 was constructed in 1904 for the express purpose of serving as the base hospital and served Fort Bliss well until the completion and opening of William Beaumont Army Hospital on September 1, 1921.

According to available records, Building 1 was originally constructed in a simplified Colonial Revival style and contains 30,340 square feet. This three story building was constructed with a limestone and stucco foundation, brick masonry walls, and slate gable and hipped roofs. The building's gabled center section is flanked by wings with hip-roofs. Both wings contain exterior concrete steps with pipe railings and exterior fire stairs for egress from the second floor. Three chimneys project above the steeply pitched roof line. The double-hung wood sash windows contain 2/2 lights and screen[87]. This historic old building, after its many years of service as a hospital, currently houses the Directorate of Resource Management[88].

According to Ms Heidi Crabtree's book[89], and also confirmed by those who work in this huge old building, there are a large number of tings that have taken place inside these walls that would certainly lead to hauntings. As a former hospital, there were, without a doubt, numerous deaths and serious illnesses treated in the wards and there are stories that a morgue once existed in the basement area. If someone dies far away from home, surrounded by strangers, is it not possible that some portion of the essence of that man would strive to remain on this earth, seeking the peace and happiness denied to him during life?

When the ghosts that occupy this building walk the darkened hallways once the living have returned to their homes make their presences known, there are those who can sense or even see the actual spirit and those that can only see the results of the spirits' passage. According to many witnesses, the front doors of the building, which face Pershing Road, have been known to open and close unaided by any living hand as if there is a regular flow of personnel in and out of the building. This decidedly unnerving event has been observed by a large number of people who were, I might add, somewhat reluctant to discuss their experiences with the unknown in any detail.

Several others of the personnel that work in this building comment that a lot of people do not want to be in this building alone. Even those who do not

---

[86] Crabtree, Heidi Veronica, An Overview of the Histories and Myths of Fort Bliss' Oldest Buildings, A Crabtree Hollow Book, 2000.

[87] National Register of Historic Places Registration Form for the Fort Bliss Main Post Historic District, 2nd Edition, November 2000.

[88] National Register of Historic Places Registration Form for the Fort Bliss Main Post Historic District, 2nd Edition, November 2000.

[89] Ibid

believe in ghosts have to admit that there is 'something' odd about this old building.

I had heard many ghost stories about Fort Bliss since moving to El Paso, but they were always general in nature. However, in spite of the many stories I have heard, the first inkling that I had about the spirits that walk the dark silent halls of Building 1 was on a Ghost Tour of Fort Bliss conducted for myself, and a few friends, by Colonel (P) Bob Lennox, his family[90] and Ms. Glenda Bromberg, wife of Brigadier General Howard Bromberg and Ms. Pam Green, wife of Major General Stanley Green, Fort Bliss Commander. Colonel Lennox was the first person to ever mention the hauntings at Building 1 to me, but he was certainly not the last.

To continue on with the strange occurrences that have been reported in and around Building 1, I have heard other stories about footsteps being heard in empty hallways. Workers in the building who have had occasion to go to the basement sometimes report detecting strong odors of formaldehyde coming from the basement area. As I mentioned earlier, I have heard from several individuals that when this building served as the base hospital, the morgue was located in the basement and this was where autopsies were conducted. Formaldehyde was used to preserve the organs and tissue samples removed from the cadavers during these procedures. Much of the unusual activity seems to revolve around the former morgue area. I suppose that it could be spirits searching for the rest of their bodies removed by the pathologists.

Other people have talked about hearing footsteps on the stairs and sensing the presence of invisible entities walking behind them up or down the staircase. As has been noted by others, the stairs are somewhat old and give off loud creaks as individuals, both visible and invisible walk on them. According to Heidi Crabtree, one employee upon reaching the top of the stairs to descend to the lower floors felt cool air brush by him as if someone or something had pushed past him.

There are some employees that refuse to work after hours for fear that they will also will have a brush with the unknown. During daylight hours, the building has a certain impression on one's senses, but nothing compared to the sensations that assault the senses after dark. The night belongs to the spirits of the restless dead.

---

[90] This Ghost Tour of Fort Bliss had been a prize in the silent auction conducted at the 2002 Air Defense Artillery Associations Gala. It cost me $150.00 to win this particular prize, but it was well worth every penny. The little known history of these old buildings related by Colonel (P) and his family as well as Glenda Bromberg and Pam Green, who both came along to help narrate the fascinating stories about this Post, was worth far more than the cost of the tour. I would have gladly paid several times that amount had it been necessary. The reader will also find pictures of Colonel Lennox and his family members, as well as Glenda Bromberg and Pam Green (Mrs. Stanley Green, Fort Bliss Commander) dressed in period costumes, throughout the book.

In the picture shown below, note the two story porch that runs across the front of the building.

Figure 17: Building 1 as original constructed.

CHAPTER EIGHT
BUILDING 4

Figure 18: Connie Wang in front of Building 4.

When I began writing this book, I discovered that there is not very much written reference material available about the many alleged hauntings on

Fort Bliss and with current security measures in place, trying to enter a locked building to look for ghosts can actually get you shot or at least detained and questioned. Most of the Military Police on Fort Bliss are hard headed, down to earth believers in what they can see, hear, taste or touch. Ghosts do not enter into their vocabulary; that is until they run into one of Fort Bliss' permanent residents. Building 4 has long been off limits to all entry, with all windows and doors boarded over with sheets of plywood as shown in the picture on the preceding page.

Building 4 is a rectangular two story building, with a fascinating basement, constructed in 1914, containing 7,321 square feet. The building is constructed with a brick foundation, water table and walls. The windows are double-hung wood sashes with 8/8 lights and screens. A single medium pitched hipped roof covers the building. The design of the building called for two porches, one on each end of the building. The original ground floor porch and second level balconies have been enclosed with wood clapboard siding. The enclosed purchased have shed roofs beginning at the eave line of the building's main body[91].

I was lucky enough, as I will explain later, to get a chance to wander through Building 4 not once, but twice, in my pursuit of elusive military ghosts. Building 4 has long had the reputation as being the most haunted building on Fort Bliss. Everyone I have talked to about ghosts and possible haunted locations on the historic old post has immediately mentioned Building Four. It was a key part of the ghost tour conducted for us by Colonel (P) Lennox and his family with somewhat unexpected consequences for both the Colonel and myself as I almost decked a "ghost" who came upon me by surprise.

As can be seen from the photograph, above left, this is one of the oldest buildings on Post and the doors and windows are securely boarded up. The outside stairs leading to the second floor are rickety and dangerous. When I first discussed writing a book about the ghosts of Fort Bliss, I was informed that Building 4 was THE haunted building on the Post and that Heidi Crabtree had written everything that there was to know about all of the haunted buildings on post. From reading her book, which is every hard to find, I also discovered that Building 4 was also THE building that started Heidi Crabtree's historical search for the history of the old buildings on post and it was the one building that I wanted a chance to get inside of and explore. However, due to Post regulations regarded boarded up buildings, it did not seem likely that I would get my chance to get inside of those old building.

According to her book[92] when she first visited building 4, Heidi Crabtree couldn't believe how badly the old building looked. With its building number

---

[91] National Register of Historic Places Registration Form for the Fort Bliss Main Post Historic District, 2nd Edition, November 2000.

[92] Crabtree, Heidi Veronica, An Overview of the Histories and Myths of Fort Bliss' Oldest Buildings, A Crabtree Hollow Book, 2000

hanging askew amidst rotten wood, green vines beginning to creep across the entrance, and leaves piled up at the base of the outside steps to the basement, it certainly looked more like a movie version of a stereotypical haunted house than a building across the street from the Headquarters of one of the largest military posts in the United States. She said that she even spotted a black widow spider in a web. Frankly, from Heidi Crabtree's description, all that was needed was a walking skeleton or the sounds of chains rattling to make the scene perfect.

Figure 19: Connie Wang and Sharon Hudnall walk alongside Building 4.

When I first saw Building 4, up close and personal, so to speak, on the Great Fort Bliss Ghost Tour, the outside stairs were rickety and closed off; the windows had long been boarded over by the Facilities Engineers and overall, the building had a general sense of abandonment about it. I didn't see a black widow spider or a spider web, but I do not doubt that there may have been one or more in the darker recesses of the darkened structure. This building may have seemed too good to be true to Ms. Crabtree, but for me it turned out to be a case of being careful what you wished for because you just may get it. At a time I least expected it, I got it; I was able to enter Building 4 and explore to my heart's content.

Turning once again to Heidi Crabtree's fascinating book, obtaining the keys from Real Property to enable her to enter the building was not a problem. She had called Jim Litzau to arrange to pick up the keys to the building and Heidi and James Crabtree, Heidi's husband, drove over to Real Property on James' lunch hour and they were able to sign the keys out[93]. When the two of them decided to enter the old building for the first time, it was early afternoon. She recorded feel that she had had invaded someone's personal space when they entered the deserted building, and based upon the many stories that I have heard, she may have been more accurate than she knew.

Heidi was not a novice at entering and exploring old abandoned structures, as she related that years before she and her friends had enjoyed finding old, abandoned buildings and houses to explore. She reported that they had even found an entrance to the Underground Railroad back in Ohio, but even that adventure was not as disturbing to her as the sensations that she felt upon entering Building 4.

In the absence of man, she reported that pigeons had taken over the building, their dropping and feathers making it very nasty place. They found bird skeletons and tons of droppings everywhere. Some of the windows, which are now boarded over, were broken from the birds, and glass shards littered the second floor. She said that there was ugly tattered carpet still covering the floor in some rooms. A file cabinet covered with bird droppings sat at the top of the stairs as if abandoned by those who had been assigned to remove it from the building. A few cat carcasses complement the ambience as well.

Heidi and James Crabtree found that the basement was very dark, even with the afternoon Texas sun blazing in the west. She remembered that they both had the shivers upon reaching the last room on the right. There had been some type of vault in this room with an ancient light bulb hanging inside. Later research revealed that this was, in fact, a vault such as is used for classified documents. Records show that this particular vault had been installed in the 1930s. There were bars on the windows down in the basement as well. The electricity was working, and as she and her husband stood in the dank, dark basement, Heidi wrote that they both distinctly heard water running somewhere in the old building.

---

[93] This was prior to the building being completely boarded up as it is now. At the time she had her adventures in Building 4, it was still in a fairly good state of repair. When I was there, I remember thinking that a good forceful sneeze might make the walls come tumbling down.

As an aside to the notion that water was heard running in the building, a common belief of those who spend any time inside this old structure, Heidi

Figure 20: Typical of the condition of the rooms inside Building 4.

commented that she and her husband could almost "feel" the water running in the walls, as if someone upstairs was running water. This interesting observation, which would ordinarily mean that there was someone else in the building, made little impression on them until much later. They snapped some photos of the basement area and that was the end of the first visit.

When Heidi took the keys to Building 4 back to Jim Litzau at Real Property, in the course of their discussion, she told him about hearing the water running in the building. She wrote that he looked incredulous because, as he told her, the water had been shut off in that building for many years. In spite of the water being shut off, Heidi would later learn that toilets had a habit of flushing by themselves and had been heard by many who worked in that building for any length of time. I am told that this was only one of the many reasons that no one wanted to work in this historic old building.

Heidi related that she talked to some former employees of Building 4, who, in return for telling their stories, requested that she not use their names. After hearing their stories, she decided to conduct some detailed research into the history of Building 4, which turned into a major headache.

According to her research, Building 4 was built as an adjunct to the Hospital in 1914 for the purpose of being used as an isolation ward. A close examination of the parking areas between Building 8, the first Hospital built on

Fort Bliss and Building 4, directly across the street from Building 8 shows that originally a walkway connected the two buildings. Building 9, the original morgue, was also connected to Building 8 by a sloping walkway. Heidi Crabtree also found that Building 4 saw use as an overflow for the morgue when necessary.

The Influenza Pandemic hit Ft Bliss and El Paso pretty hard back in the autumn of 1918. The number of deaths in the El Paso area was tremendous and the huge amount of dead bodies overwhelmed the public facilities. In El Paso, as discussed in *Spirits of the Border: The History and Mystery of El Paso Del Norte*[94], the bodies that could not be maintained in the local morgue were wrapped and stored in the basement of El Paso High School. At Fort Bliss, since local facilities were already filled to overflowing, the bodies of the dead were stored in the basements of several Post buildings, and from what I have been told, Building 4 being one of them.

Due to the hot weather common in the Southwest, the Army constructed the original buildings at fort Bliss in a style similar to tropical billets found on military posts such as Fort Clayton in the Panama Canal Zone. The first floor is left open for air circulation and there are a number of open air balconies such as were originally part of Building 4's design. Heidi Crabtree felt that victims of tuberculosis, or consumption as it was called back then, were placed here. Any soldier who had a contagious, and often deadly, disease would have been walked, wheeled, or carried into Building 4 as its original purpose was as an isolation ward. She was not able to find any floor plans of the building built in the teens, but she believed that there may have been an autopsy room located in the basement.

In the 1930s Building 4 ceased to serve as an isolation ward and entered a period of being used by several different entities at the same time. Housed within its walls during this time period were a walk-in dispensary, a dental clinic, an X-ray room, and a VD clinic. Heidi mentioned that she had bought an old Ft Bliss telephone directory from 1958 in which Building 4 is listed as a dispensary, so it seems to have served this purpose for over two decades.

From everything that I can discover, Heidi Crabtree was and is a very careful investigator. She would not just take the word of a single individual that a particular building was haunted, but talked to everyone she could find who had had any contact with the building in question. So it was in regard to Building 4. According to her book, she spoke with people who had worked in this building at various times from the 1970s into the 1990s. She confirmed that none of the people that she had told to had talked to each other or even known each other, so when similar stories were unearthed, she realized that something strange was taking place in regard to Building 4. She discovered that three different apparitions, at least, had been spotted several times.

---

[94] Hudnall, Ken and Connie Wang, Spirits of the Border: The History and Mystery of El Paso Del Norte, Omega Press, El Paso, Texas. 2003.

The first story she reported dealt with an incident that took place near Christmas some years ago. She was told that a female employee working in Building 4 had decided to stay late after work to make some Christmas decorations for the offices. Late that afternoon, the employee was alone in the basement, sitting quietly, making wreaths out of the old punch-style IBM cards that the US Military appeared to be so fond of. For no reason that she could put name to, she glanced up toward the door.

To her surprise, she caught sight of a man in what she described as a very old military uniform. She could see cavalry boots visible beneath the white lab type jacket that he was wearing. She could not see the man's face since he wore a white surgical mask covering his lower face. Though Heidi Crabtree did not mention it in her book, in the version of the story that I was told as the startled woman watched, the figure seemed to fade away. Unnerved, vanishing figures were certainly not part of her job description, she dropped her work, grabbed her things, and fled the building.

Another story that I have heard from several sources, to include Heidi Crabtree's fascinating book[95] involved another female government employee that worked in a neighboring building. One afternoon she was on her way to her car that was parked near Building 4. As she passed the south side of that historic old building she took notice of a young woman in a bright blue Flapper style dress and a matching hat, standing outside the building as if she was waiting for ride. According to this witness, the young woman didn't move, but simply stared straight ahead.

The employee unlocked her car, placed her briefcase in the backseat, but was struck by the impulse to turn and look again at the silent Blue Lady. To her surprise, the young woman had vanished. Heidi Crabtree also wrote that an employee with Public Affairs[96] reported that her young daughter had seen the Blue Lady as they drove down Slater Rd late one night after attending a show. The daughter commented that it was odd to see a woman standing outside a desert building that late at night, but her mother didn't see the ghost.

Heidi wrote that she was taken aback not long ago. She had stopped off at the building that housed Public Affairs to pick up a copy of The Monitor[97], and was surprised to see a car parked outside of Building 4 as it was rather late. Not being what one would call shy, Heidi said that she walked over to investigate, thinking that she had come upon some vandals. Instead, she wrote that she found two soldiers who claimed they were from Holloman Air Force Base. They told her that they had heard the stories about the ghosts in Building 4 and had come to see if they could see one. Heidi reported that their wives sat frightened in the

---

[95] Crabtree, Heidi Veronica, An Overview of the Histories and Myths of Fort Bliss' Oldest Buildings, A Crabtree Hollow Book, 2000
[96] The Public Affairs Office is not very far from Building 4.
[97] The Monitor is the current name of the Fort Bliss newspaper and its' offices share a building with the Public Affairs office.

back seat of the car. Apparently they did not share their husbands' enthusiasm for ghost hunting.

Figure 21: The Woman in Blue? - It's Katelyn Hobson on the steps at the rear of Building 4. Glenda Bromberg Watches from Door.

When Heidi said that she was the one doing the writing about the ghosts that they were referring to, they told her the experience that one of their friends, stationed at Fort Bliss, had experienced at Building 4. According to the story, this friend, his wife, and daughter went to Building 4 to "ghost hunt" a short time before and apparently found more than they bargained for as they were terrified and run out of the building by something they had not seen, but clearly it had seen them.

The intrepid soldier and his wife went into the building via the basement on a spur of the moment ghost hunt, leaving their young daughter sitting in the car. As they were climbing the stairs from the basement to the first floor they both heard a voice say, "They're going upstairs" and then another voice say, "Help me move this." This was followed by a dragging noise from the basement! The couple had just completed thoroughly exploring the basement and knew that there was no one was down there.

Completely unnerved by this unexpected turn of events, the couple abandoned their ghost hunt, ran back down the stairs into the basement, and exited the building as fast as humanly possible. They made no effort to discover the source of the voices. The two jumped into their car and according to the story, the soldier in getting away from that building certainly broke post speed laws and possibly land speed records.

The two soldiers told Heidi that once a semblance of calm returned to the car, the daughter asked her parents who the woman was that she had seen standing outside the building while her parents had been inside looking for ghosts. The girl's farther snapped that he neither knew nor cared who the woman was. Later, puzzled at his daughter's comment about a woman standing outside the building, as neither he nor his wife had seen anyone outside the building when they entered and left, asked her to describe what she had seen. She replied that she had seen a woman in a blue dress standing outside the building while her parents had been inside.

Heidi wrote about another instance when she was passing Building 4 and saw the same soldiers outside the building. She stopped and they told her that they wanted to go inside the building through the basement. Clearly not an individual who will pass up an adventure, Heidi Crabtree went inside the basement with them. The intrepid band of explorers had just explored the "vault room" and stepped back into the hall when they heard the ancient doorbell ring long and loud. In the normal course of events a doorbell ringing is not an event that can be considered earth shaking as doorbells are designed to ring, but in this instance it was certainly strange. You see the electricity to Building 4 was turned off long ago and I am told that the old doorbell has been rusted and inoperable for many years. Was this the ghost asking them to leave or perhaps the Lady in the Blue Dress wanting to come inside?

The story of the third apparition haunting the building comes from a time when the building was still in use. According to the story, this mysterious figure was spotted one afternoon as the witness was preparing to leave work for the day. The witness said that he was alone in the building, and since it was late in the day, he was on his way out as well. He said that he stepped out of his second floor office into the hall and froze in his tracks. He could very clearly see the gray misty figure of a man was standing at the window on the north side. The figure had its back to the frightened man and seemed to pay him no attention; the figure just stood, staring out of the window.

The employee said that he ducked back into his office and waited. Finally, the tension was too much as he cautiously peeped around out his office door and into the hall. He could not see the figure any longer and decided that this would be a good time to exit himself. He then made himself scarce as well!

As of the time she wrote her book in 2000, one of the latest apparition stories involving Building 4 actually happened to her husband, James Crabtree, although she says that he doesn't boast about it. As with most husbands of adventurous wives, Heidi reports that he is very disturbed by her and her group entering this place, and will not attend our hunts. At least, she said, not after what he saw this past February.

According to the story that James Crabtree told his wife, it was a warm night, with a big full moon. James decided to take an evening bicycle ride. Heidi said that rather than join him, she settled back to "surf the net" while he was gone. She said that she was excited when he returned, having had an email from a former MP who relayed some wonderful stories about Building 117 and the Post cemetery to her. James was red- faced, looking like he gave himself a good workout, and she paid no attention to anything, and just babbled on about this new contact. It was when she finally shut up that he told her that he had seen something.

Figure 22: Building 4 as it was when it was in use[98].

She was so surprised that she asked him to repeat that, and he caught his breath and told her the following story. He said that he had biked down Pershing and used the large parking lot on Slater to turn around. He said that he just wanted to see if any lights were on in Building 4, as the lights had a habit of turning themselves on and off. As he looked toward Building 4, he said that he saw a man with an old Cavalry type uniform, wearing a long white lab coat, and wearing an old fashioned Stetson hat. He said that the figure was distinctly walking towards either Building 2[99] or Building 1[100]. He said that he blinked and looked again, but the figure had vanished.

---

[98] This picture came to me courtesy of Susan Payne, Archivist with the Fort Bliss directorate of Environment.
[99] Building 2 is the current Post Headquarters.
[100] Building 1 was originally the second Post Hospital and now houses JAG.

Heidi said that not everyone who has been inside or around Building 4 gets to see a ghost. More common manifestations are sounds such as voices and ghostly footsteps. She also reported that objects in the building also seem to have minds of their own[101]. She said that these incidents became so common that this is the reason that the building was finally abandoned and the military offices moved elsewhere. Score one for the ghosts!

I must point out that no one that I spoke to about the reason Building 4 was abandoned would confirm that it was due to ghostly activity, but it would certainly explain why a building less than a 100 yards from the Post Headquarters sits empty and dark. I might also add that while no one would confirm that ghosts had caused the abandonment of Building 4, no one would go so far as to deny that ghosts had chased the military out of the building either.

Heidi also reported another story of spooky happenings inside Building

Figure 23: Second floor inside Building 4, Glenda Bromberg pictured at rear.

4. She said that an employee came by one weekend before Building 4 was abandoned, having left some important papers lying on his desk rather than placing them in the safe as required. He brought his wife along with him, and while they were upstairs he heard loud music begin to play in one of the other offices on that floor. He told his wife to find and shut off the radio that was

---

[101] I have also heard a number of stories about things disappearing and reappearing inside this old building.

playing. She found the radio that was merrily playing away, but when she tried to turn it off, she found that it would not turn off. She went to unplug it and discovered that it was already unplugged. She called her husband and he decided to remove the batteries, but when he tried to remove the batteries, he found to his shock that there WERE no batteries in it! The mysterious radio was still playing merrily as they left the building.

Both Heidi Crabtree and several Military Police officers that I know, report that MPs have made numerous trips to this old building to shut off the lights that had somehow turned on.

Though Heidi's adventures would have been more than enough for most people, she was not ready to run from a mere ghost. The next time she signed out the keys to Building 4, she and her husband walked around more carefully, noting whatever we could. This was still long before James Crabtree had his run in with the figure wearing the old Cavalry Uniform and the Stetson outside Building 4. They took more photos, and she reported that she snapped one last shot of the north side of the building as we left.

She said that when the film was developed, James noticed an orangey light in one of the windows. Irregularly shaped, she was sure that this odd light was not there when they took the photo. She said that the sun was behind the mountains so it obviously was not sunlight. Three photo experts have looked at the picture, as well as the negative, but, she said, they couldn't explain it. Heidi said that scanning the picture shows that the object in the picture is three dimensional, not flat against the wall in that room.

Heidi said that she and her husband eagerly showed the building to a friend from California, SSGT Tom Murotake from the 40th Infantry (MECH) Division. As they showed him through the building, as we stood upstairs, a door on the first floor slammed shut. Not knowing what to make of a door slamming in an empty building, they decided that it was just the wind. But, she implied that none of them though it had been the wind.

· Though Heidi's writing shows that she had accomplished a lot while her husband was stationed at Fort Bliss, when James Crabtree left in July of 1999 for a five month rotation, she said that the ghost hunts moved to high gear. She said that she had to do something with my free time. So she made arrangements with Joanne Shaw of the El Paso Tour Company to take a few friends and a psychic into Building 4.

It was during this period that she said that she met Edward Weissbard, who would become a partner in crime! She said that the group met at a Japanese restaurant for lunch and then carpooled over to Building 4. The psychic brought by Joanne Shaw was none other than Connie Wang, a good friend of mine.

Connie Wang, my co-author in *Spirits of the Border: The History and Mystery of El Paso Del Norte*[102] and in this book as well is an accomplished

---

[102]Hudnall, Ken and Connie Wang, Spirits of the Border: The History and Mystery of El Paso Del Norte, Omega Press, El Paso, Texas. 2003.

psychic. Coincidentally, she was the psychic that Joanne Shaw brought to Building 4 to work with Heidi. Connie told me about her adventures in Building 4 with Heidi Crabtree and company. She is convinced that there are many presences inside of Building 4, but she does not feel that they are malevolent. She told me that based on that visit to Building 4 that she was convinced that something was in the basement. She said that she picked out one spot in the basement and told the others that there was something there.

Connie said that the group rolled up the frayed carpet and saw nothing. She still insisted that something was there, so she said that Heidi used a car key to pry up a floor tile, to find a filled in drain which was about 6 inches or so in diameter. Connie said that from the moment that they uncovered that drain, that the room has smelled foul. In discussions with me during the preparation of this book, she said that the moment the drain was uncovered she sensed great evil and danger emanating from that small outlet. She said that it was the main outlet for the autopsy room. As each body was opened, the fluids from the bodies ran from the tables down into the drain. Could it be that with the fluids went essences such as good or evil?

However, the big even that I have heard so much about were the plans made to do an in-depth investigation of Building 4, on Halloween night 1999. Heidi wrote that Jim at Real Property thought she and the rest of the group were crazy to want to spend the night in that old drafty rat infested building, but he gave her the keys anyway.

As might be expected with her natural exuberance and enthusiasm, Heidi was the first one of the group to arrive, but she wrote that she was about to enter the darkened building alone. She said that she had come prepared for anything. She had a large plastic skeleton propped into the convertible, along with 35mm camera equipment, a Polaroid, a throwaway camera, a video camera, tripods, coffee pot, Halloween candy, and some WWI era Army books to "spur" anything on, and two folding director style chairs. Edward showed up later with food and soda, camera equipment, a TV with VCR, and his young cousin.

Another sergeant and his wife came along a little later, and we set up a video camera in the basement and another on the second floor. After having cased the place to make sure that no one was inside, and to insure that they had run the pigeons off, Heidi reported that they settled back in one of the rooms by the front door. She said that they chatted a bit, keeping it low so as not to make noise that might be picked up by the video cameras. Heidi said that according to her notes, the fun began at about 6:30pm.

She said that they all heard soft footsteps moving about upstairs, though

Figure 24: Basement Hallway in Building 4. "Vault Room" is at end of this hallway.

they knew that there was no one (nothing human, that it) upstairs. It was still daylight outside so they were not frightened yet. At 6:50 the sound of loud footsteps stomping down the stairs from the upper floors caused all conversation to cease. The sounds were coming from stairs that were just on the other side of the wall from where the group was sitting. Heidi wrote that she would never forget the expression on the face of the sergeant who was standing in the doorway leading to the stairs! She said that all of their eyes were as big as saucers, and she, for one, was convinced that something was about to walk around the corner and into our room. The Sergeant standing in the doorway turned around, but nothing was there. They never found out whom or what was making the sounds of someone stomping down the stairs.

After being in shock, she said for about half a minute, they all grabbed

Figure 25: This artwork, as fresh and vivid as the day it was painted, is in the stairwell.

their cameras and stepped out of the room. The stairs were right in front of them, and she said that they all snapped photos. She also said that Edward's electromagnetic frequency meter was screaming! Heidi said that they can all be heard on her videotape that night saying, "Hello? Hello?" up the stairs!

After this, the five of them, went back to the room in which they were "camping" and then, when it was suggested that they should go outside for a smoke to insure that any noises they made were not picked up by the cameras. She makes the comment that it was quite cold outside, and that they routinely smoked indoors anyway, being careful of course by bringing a water can to dispose of the butts in. She also makes the comment that the fact that they stayed outside for almost an hour showed that they were just plain scared. Heidi also made the comment that even though she had quit smoking she went through two packs of cigarettes that night.

Heidi said that it was hard on them to go upstairs to check on her camera's battery, but it needed recharging or it would have been useless. However, when they got to the basement, she said that they received a big surprise. When they arrived in the basement area, they found that Edward's camera refused to stay on. He had it wired through the VCR that was plugged into the wall, which eliminating the need for battery changes and reliance upon short one hour tapes. However, they would turn it on but when they checked back

10 minutes later, the camera would always be shut off. As a result of the camera shutting itself off, they were not able to get any footage of any activity that might have occurred in the basement that night.

She said that the same thing happened with the audio tape recorder in the basement and at one point, the machine even refused to record. The buttons would not operate no matter what they tried, but she said that as soon as they took it back to their main room, the recorder worked perfectly.

About 9:30 the sergeant and his wife had left. The three that were left were literally shaking. They all felt that, as Heidi put it, "something was about to give" and so they collected our equipment and left by 11:00. Who knows what might have happened at the "Witching Hour."

Heidi said that Edward phoned a few days later to see if she had watched her videotapes of that night, and she told him that she hadn't. Heidi wrote that she honestly didn't look forward to watching hours and hours of a tape recording of an empty hallway. However, she said that she did finally sit down to watch the tapes one evening a week later, and after a short time, she said, she had to turn the TV off and call Edward. She said that there was something unexplainable on this tape and she was too scared to watch it alone. He came over the next evening and they sat, eating brownies, to watch it.

On the tape, wrote Heidi, there is a definite interference that begins at about 6:30 and disappears, only to reoccur throughout the first tape. They found that each time the interference occurs a peculiar metallic pounding is heard. The strangest part is that at no time while they were there did they actually hear this metallic pounding. She said that the boots storming down the steps that had spooked them into going outside for an hour long smoke cannot be heard on the tapes, but when the volume is turned up all the way, shouting can be heard.

Both Edward and Heidi agreed that none of them had been shouting! "Beeping" is also heard at one point on the tape, and on tape two, the interference is so bad that the view actually goes completely black at times. Another oddity is that a grunt or throat clearing sound is heard right next to the microphone, and something taps the microphone a few times just like a speaker will tape a microphone to see if the microphone is "live" before beginning a talk.

In an attempt to try and identify the mysterious doctor seen by several people to include her husband, Heidi went through the post returns for Ft Bliss in the teens, and came up with a list of doctors who were stationed here from 1914-1916.

According to what she found, Lieutenant Colonel Paul F Straub was commander of the Post Hospital in 1916. At this point in time, the Post Hospital would have been what is now designated as Building 1. She actually found a picture of this man, which she said that she posted to her website. However, she also wrote that she found one doctor that really intrigued her, Captain Louis Caspar Duncan.

According to the records, he arrived at Fort Bliss from Washington Barracks in 1913. During his tour of duty at Fort Bliss, in addition to his medical duties, he also found the time to write at least one book, entitled "*The Medical Department of the United States in the Civil War.*"

The book has been reprinted by Olde Soldier Books, and Heidi obtained a copy through the mail. She found that in addition to being a physician and an author, that Duncan also had some artistic talent, for he did the illustrations for his book as well. A through search of website references also enabled Heidi to get a certain insight into this man of many talents.

Captain Louis Caspar Duncan was born in 1869, and joined the Army in March of 1898, just in time for the Spanish-American War. Being from St. Petersburg, Florida, which was the embarkation point for US forces[103] being shipped out to Cuba and Puerto Rico, he was readily taken. Judging by his age, it is very probable that Caspar Duncan was most likely already a doctor upon joining the military. There is no question that he was a very intelligent student of military history based upon his many accomplishments of letters.

However, whatever may have been his status upon joining the military he was certainly a military medical doctor by 1912. In that year, Captain Duncan visited Gettysburg, and submitted a report and design for tablets to mark the locations of the Hospitals of the Army of the Potomac. He won a Seaman Prize for his paper "*Comparative Mortality of Disease and Battle Casualties in the Historic Wars of the World.*" He would later write "*Medical Men in the American Revolution.*"

While he was here at Ft Bliss he served as the Medical Corps Recruiting Officer in 1914, and was the Post Surgeon from November 1914 to January 1915, when Captain Duncan was replaced by a Major McAndrew. In October of 1915 Captain Duncan spent 4 months in Sierra Blanca with Second Lieutenant named George Patton! Duncan was promoted to-the rank of Major on August 22, 1916 and was assigned duty at the Fort Bliss base hospital, then Building 1.

Unfortunately, all post returns ended at December 1916 so Heidi could not trace any more info on this man. She contacted the National Personnel Records Center in St Louis, MO for any addition information on Captain Duncan, but was informed that he his service date ended in 1921. The only other information available was that he returned to St Petersburg, and died there in 1940.

Though Captain Duncan's accomplishments set him apart as a very erudite, accomplished officer, he and his work is all but forgotten. Each of us is given a certain period of time in which to make our mark and Captain Duncan made his almost a century ago. As is the way of all men, his works now fade into the mists of time, to be replaced by the accomplishments and exploits of others. Is Captain Duncan the mysterious Cavalry Officer many have seen in and around Building 4? Based upon his history of dedication, it could be that he is still here

---

[103] Teddy Roosevelt and his Rough Riders also spent some time in St. Petersburg and in "Old Town" there are a number of stories about some of their "non-military" activities. Let's just say that they were not called the Rough Riders for nothing.

wanting to treat the ill, only his patients died over 100 years ago. Only the dead know for sure the identity of this mysterious commanding figure and they do not seemed disposed to talk to those of us who have not yet joined them.

Heidi Crabtree had spent a great deal of time digging into the past of Building 4 and it was time to get on with other adventures. But, just when she thought that she was finally through with the ghosts of Building 4, she met some soldiers who were just as interested in ghosts as she was.

One of these soldiers was Specialist Jennifer Grey, a young lady who wasn't a believer in ghosts until she experienced the specters inside Building 4. She and some friends from the Public Affairs Office went inside that silent, deserted building one night; they had tried to call Heidi to invite her but Heidi and her husband were in San Antonio that weekend.

The intrepid ghost hunters had taken a video camera and continually filmed their movements through the building. Later, they saw with much surprise, that as the camera ran, and one of the girls seemed to disappear for a second as she was filmed walking down the hall. One evening as Specialist Grey and some MP acquaintances approached Building 4 from the north they spotted an eerie glow in the same window in which Heidi's phenomena-photo occurred. This light slowly enlarged, then became two lights, and then it was gone. Heidi also heard of a couple of MPs who, responding to a possible prowler call, were in the building, on the stairs, when they heard voices coming from a place that they had just inspected. They nearly shot themselves getting out, as they had their weapons drawn!

Specialist Grey and Heidi, along with some others, decided to spend another night in Building 4. As before, they placed video cameras about the building to record anything that might happen. One camera was in the basement and the other was placed on the top floor. As the group sat in the dark, footsteps were heard, and the atmosphere was incredibly creepy, but nothing significant was happening.

Apparently becoming a little bored, Heidi and Captain Jacquelyn Hellmeier wandered down to the fire station to ask about their ghosts. Upon returning to Building 4, they found that everyone was outside. It seemed that they group had all gone upstairs-to check on the camera and "orbs" of light were seen floating up and down the hall.

While they were discussing these orbs, another couple of people showed up and wanted to go inside Building 4. Heidi and her group remained outside, and it wasn't long before this couple rushed out, saying that they had just seen someone in the basement, and it appeared as though the white figure was reaching its hand out toward them as if it wanted something. This made Heidi's group's hair stand on end as, earlier, according to Heidi, someone in the group had seen the same thing on the first floor.

Captain Hellmeier and a few others wandered up to the second floor, and just stood at the top of the stairs, waiting for anything to happen when a door in the middle of the hall closed by itself. There are two doors in the hall dividing it, and one just went from open to shut even though there was no wind. This incident is preserved on videotape as well. Heidi also wrote that when they reviewed the tapes streaks of light can be seen shooting through the basement that were not seen by the naked eye.

The last time Heidi entered Building 4 was in May of 2000. She had sworn that she would never go back after what happened that night. It was very late and Heidi and her companions had to, once again, climb the rickety exterior steps to the top floor. It was nearly time for the tape in the video camera that they had earlier placed on the floor to run out. Seven of the group decided to stand up there, in total darkness, just watching for anything that might happen[104].

One by one the members of the group noticed something incredible. Visible in the viewfinder on this night-vision camera were lights, balls of light, traveling up the hall, down the hall, on the floor, walls and ceiling. These lights did not "bend" when they crossed open doorways; they seemed solid. They came at us from the end of the hall, and shot out from right next to the group. The most unusual thing was that they balls of light were not visible to the onlookers by just looking down the hall with their own eyes; the incredible orbs of lights could only be seen by looking through the viewfinder of the camera. The night vision capabilities of the camera made the balls of light visible. After watching the light show for fifteen or twenty minutes, Heidi and her group packed up their equipment and left the building for the final time.

---

[104] The electricity in Building 4 had been shut off earlier in 2001.

THE GREAT FORT BLISS GHOST TOUR
REACHES BUILDING 4

On the Great Fort Bliss Ghost Tour, Colonel (P) Bob Lennox told us

Figure 26: Colonel (P) Lennox (R), in period costume, made the tour a family affair. The two younger men, also in period clothing are his sons, escorting Glenda Bromberg, wife of BG Howard Bromberg.

some of the many stories of the spirits that walk this old building while standing beside the darkened Building 4. I might also add that night had fallen and even the few street lights did not add much of a glow to the area. I was standing near Glenda Bromberg when I made the comment that it was too bad that we could not go inside the building. I spoke a bit too soon.

It was a soft January evening, not too cold and not exactly warm. The tour was conducted on foot as we walked (I limped) from building to building in the area around Building 2. The schedule called for us to go to a number of buildings and end up at the Pershing House for hot cider and stories regarding the hauntings in that historic old home.

Walking over to the stairs that descend into the basement, Glenda noticed

Figure 27: These two lovely ladies are Pam Green (L), wife of MG Stanley Green and Mrs. Lennox, wife of Col. (P) Bob Lennox.

that someone had kicked a hole in the plywood that had covered the entrance to the dark, silent basement, the basement where so many had seen and heard so much. She looked at me and made the comment that the door was open and there was no reason not to take up the invitation. With that she, long skirt and all, walked down the steps, carefully stepped through the hole and vanished into the darkness. I glanced around and it seemed as if everyone was watching me to see if a crippled[105], former Infantry Captain was going to refuse to enter the breech when the tiny[106] wife of a Brigadier General had entered as if walking into a drawing room. As some other fool once said, "Damn the ghosts, uh, the torpedoes. Full speed a head!" Following her lead, I am sorry to say, I stepped through the hole in the plywood and entered darkness so intense, that it was hard to see your hand in front of your face[107].

A few feet inside the entryway, I found a doorway through which spilled a dim light. I found it fascinating that I was seeing a dim light in a building that had not had any electricity in over two years. Many of us had flashlights, in fact I

---

[105] I am a 100% disabled veteran and walk with a cane.

[106] Glenda Bromberg is a petite, attractive woman who apparently has no back up in her.

[107] As many of the group slowly followed me, Colonel (P) Lennox glanced at my wife and made the comment that it was the first time in his military career that he had totally lost control of the situation. He had laid out a meticulous program, including figures dressed in period costume to give information at various locations around main post.

had one, but this was not a light thrown by a flashlight. It was coming from a

Figure 28: This is the machine that always has a light burning on its' side even though there is no power in the building.

light on the side of a small machine set in the middle of the basement floor.

I found Glenda Bromberg standing by the machine, looking at it in a bemused manner. When I joined her she made the comment that the light I could see burning brightly was always on even though there was absolutely no power running to the building or to the machine in question. No one has ever been able to explain the light, nor what the machine was that it was sitting on.

As the others slowly joined us, I slowly moved toward the entrance to the room, seeing that this was the only way out of this particular section of the basement and it would be fewer steps for me as we moved to explore the rest of the building. I leaned in the doorway listening to the others talking when I suddenly felt someone behind me. I glanced around to see who was literally beside me in the darkened basement and got what certainly rates up there as the shock of my life.

I was fairly familiar with the history of this old building and I had just heard Colonel (P) Lennox talk about the various ghosts that had been seen in the building by others, so it was fresh on my mind. In my military career I have been in many locations and in many situations where fear is certainly a factor, but what I saw literally caused me to pause in sheer disbelief rather. Standing almost beside me was a compact figure wearing a period Cavalry Officer's Uniform, complete from the high cavalry boots on his feet to the famous white Stetson on

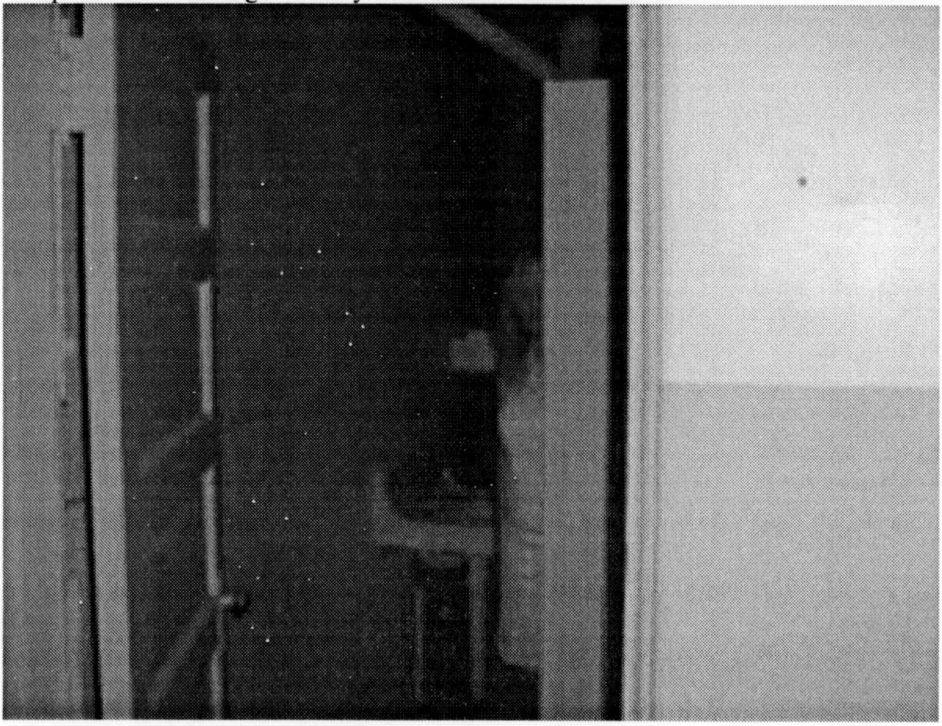

Figure 29: One of the rooms in the basement. A figure can be seen just inside the door.

his head. I was looking directly at the spectral figure described by so many and I wasn't seeing him from a distance. No, in fact, this mysterious figure and I were literally nose to nose. How's standing nose to nose with a ghost for jump starting your pacemaker?

When I began to breath again, I drew back to give this figure that had appeared by at my side as if by magic, a good old fashion cane up side the head. When I had been commissioned all those years ago, my very first Platoon Sergeant had once told me, when in doubt and out numbered hit the biggest and run. Well, I was certainly in doubt and in my mind one ghost outnumbered all of us, so I fully intended to see if I could lay out a ghost with a government issued cane and then exit the area of operations with all dispatch. I intended to let the others get out as best they could while I summoned reinforcements.

All that stopped me from proceeding to start a brawl in the basement of a haunted government building in the middle of one of the oldest military installations in the country was the "ghost" sticking out his hand and introducing himself. He was the Sergeant Major that worked for Colonel (P) Lennox and was part of the planned presentation. I never told him how close he came to getting knocked into the next week. When he had failed to show up for his part of the performance, he came looking for the tour. The rest of our group waiting outside had suggested he come into the building and find us.

Figure 30: We followed Glenda Bromberg down the dark hallway in the basement toward the stairs. No one has figured out where the light in front of her is coming from[108].

Since we had come this far, Glenda suggested that we take the grand tour. Having not seen a ghost to this point, other than my encounter with a First Sergeant dressed like a ghost, the group was certainly in favor of searching the building. So, as shown in the picture above, we followed Glenda Bromberg down the narrow basement hallway toward the stairwell.

The old building was dark and silent as we made out way from floor to floor, fragments of glass crunching beneath out feet from broken windows. Only a glimmer of the building's former grandeur was visible to us. As we ascended the dark stairwell, I was surprised to see the vivid artwork on the walls of the stairway[109] was as distinctive as the day it had been painted. Even though everything else in the building was worn and faded, these symbols of past military associations were clear and distinctive. It was a puzzle to me then and it is just as big a mystery to me now how these expertly drawn unit symbols could stay so new looking. Perhaps the building itself protected these few remaining relics of its military past.

---

[108] Anything in any of these photos that I took that night that appears to show lighted areas is coming from the flash on my camera.
[109] See page 56.

In our zeal to explore the unknown, we boldly went were few had gone in several years. The building was in a sad state of repair as shown by this photo.

Figure 31: The second floor room where Glenda Bromberg and I smelled the strong, distinctive odor of cinnamon.

To Glenda Bromberg and me the trip to the second floor[110] of the old building had some unexpected results. As we cautiously explored the dark abandoned rooms, something in the atmosphere seemed to change. To be the atmosphere had initially seemed dead, lacking even the normal warmth felt in Texas buildings, however, suddenly, Glenda and I were engulfed in a strong odor of cinnamon. It came out of nowhere and seemed to vanish as quickly. No one else in out intrepid little band reported detecting any strange odors. Search as we might, neither Glenda nor I could find anything in the building that could account for the odor.

Throughout the entire time we were in the building, I had the distinct impression that we were unconsciously waiting on something extraordinary to happen. I for one had suddenly developed a feeling of anticipation, like kid waiting for Christmas. Strangely, the feeling of anticipation that had suddenly pervaded the deserted old building seemed to me to be growing stronger. I really didn't want to know what we were anticipating, but it felt like it was going to be something to remember. I was surprised that few of the others seemed to show

---

[110] To avoid confusion, this was the second floor above the basement. Some would call this the third floor, so take your choice.

any concern over the changing atmosphere, so I did not mention anything to them. Luckily, I think, we finished this particular tour of this silent old building shortly after this, but this was not to be my last trip into the dark mysterious Building 4.

Figure 32: This photo was taken by me during the Great Fort Bliss Ghost Tour. Notice the bright light in the upper right corner f the picture. This light has never been satisfactorily explained.

GLENDA BROMBERG'S STORY REGARDING BUILDING 4

Several months after the night of the Great Ghost Tour and our impromptu tour of Building 4, I sat down with Brigadier General and Mrs. Bromberg to record their memories of unusual events on Fort Bliss. I had seen some of Glenda's events talked about in another book, but the little bit of her story that she had previously related to me did not sound exactly as I had read. I wanted to get to the truth of the matter.

On 11 July 2003, we sat in her dining room and discussed the various stories that she had heard while at Fort Bliss. She said that 3 years previously on the night of her farewell party from the 11th Brigade, as the evening wore down, there were finally only 4 people had been left. There was Glenda Bromberg, and three other officers' wives, whose names were Barb, Chris and Kathy.

It was late when they entered the van to drive home, but Glenda asked if they would like to go to a haunted house. Barb was fully in favor of the unexpected side trip while Kathy and Chris were less enthusiastic about the venture. In fact, Glenda was asked not to talk about haunted houses because it was freaking out Kathy.

When they arrived at Building 4, Glenda and Barb started up the steps to the top floor of Building 4, while Chris and Kathy refused to get out of the van. Glenda said that when she and Barb got to the top floor, where the children had been cared for, the door opened with a creaking sound like that of a haunted house. Cautiously, Glenda peered inside and decided that it looked safe enough, so she cautiously entered the littered room. Slowly, she walked down the hallway, pausing at the entrance to one of the rooms.

As she waited for her friend, she suddenly heard a sound to her left. She looked toward the window that faced toward the west. The room, though dark, was somewhat illuminated due to street lights burning outside[111]. As she hesitated, deciding what to do next, she heard a sound similar to that of a cat jumping from the window sill to the floor and then sounds like the cat was walking across the floor. However, her eyes told her that there was nothing living in the room. So she decided that perhaps it had gotten out of the room before she had seen it and run out of the building through the open door where her friend was waiting.

Puzzled, Glenda returned to the entrance and asked her friend, Barb, who had prudently elected to remain at the entrance door, if an animal had run out of the building. When Barb told her that nothing had left the building, Glenda decided they should leave, so they went back down the outside staircase to the ground level.

Seeing their two friends were still sitting timidly in the car, Glenda suggested that they pretend to go into the basement and then come up as if something had scared them in order to play a prank on their friends. So the two of them went to the steps leading to the basement and as they descended bent their knees so that they appeared to be going all the way into the basement. The area at the bottom of the steep steps was pitch black, so they were careful not to actually enter the basement.

With the stage set, Glenda told Barb that at the count of three, they would run up the steps screaming in fear. At Barb's agreement, Glenda softly counted to three and the two of them went tearing up the steps screaming at the top of their lungs. Chris and Kathy, waiting in the van did not stop to ask what had taken place, but they burned rubber getting away from the building leaving Glenda and Barb standing outside the building. It was only when the van had gone about a 100 yards that the two stopped to wait for their friends.

Glenda and barb caught up with the van, to find that the two that had remained in the vehicle were so scared that Kathy was in Chris's lap. When Glenda and Barb got seated, but before anything could be said, Chris demanded to know why the two of them had been moving boxes around in the darkened

---

[111] This was before the windows were boarded over, so even though they were filthy, the windows allowed in some light.

basement of the old building. Glenda assured her friends that neither she nor Barb had been moving any boxes in the basement, that they hadn't rally gone into the basement, but had been playing a trick on them. Then Glenda immediately demanded to know what Chris was talking about.

Chris, with Kathy helping, told Glenda and Barb that they had very clearly heard them banging and moving about in the basement of Building 4. There was no doubt, in their minds, that the two women had been moving boxes about because they could distinctly hear the scrape of the boxes being pushed and dragged across the concrete floor of the basement. Strangely, while Chris and Kathy could hear the sounds very clearly from their places in the van, Glenda and Barb, crouched at the bottom of the steps leading to the basement heard nothing. This oddity was never explained as no one wanted to go back inside the building, so it was decided that it was time for the four of them to go home. Both Glenda and I had heard several stories about people hearing boxes being moved in the basement and a related earlier, one couple even heard voices associated with the moving boxes[112].

On another evening, about 2 years ago, Glenda, Nadine Woods and Lisa DeAntonio decided to go ghost hunting inside Building 4. The three of them arrived at the deserted building and found things dark and quiet. Deciding to continue their explorations, they went into the basement, but it was so completely dark that they could see nothing. So it was decided that they would go get some flashlights and return to continue their explorations.

Returning with flashlights, the three of them began to explore the building, starting in the basement and working their way upwards to the third level. During the ascent, none of the three of them saw or heard anything out of the ordinary. However, on the way back down the stairs it was quite another story.

When they descended the stairs, all was silent and still until they reached the landing of the second floor. In some confusion, they stopped in their tracks at the sight of a small chair that was sitting in the middle of the landing. The three intrepid explorers were all sure that they had not seen that chair sitting on the second floor landing as they had made their way up the stairs. Since the landing was so small, they all knew that there was no way that the chair could have been sitting there as they went up the stairs without them seeing it.

---

[112] Just to clarify the matter, there are not now boxes or crates in the basement of this building and there have not been any boxes or crates in the basement of this building for a long, long time.

Figure 33: Glenda Bromberg standing by the chair that seems to move around the building[113].

Still moving cautiously, but somewhat faster, the three left the building and sat down on the curb to talk about the mysterious moving chair. They were all sure that the chair had not been on the landing as they had climbed the stairs from floor to floor. Finally, Nadine decided that she was going to return to the building and look at that chair one more time. She wanted to see if it was possible to cross the landing without seeing the chair.

Glenda and Lisa waited for their friend for a long time until finally she came out of the building, walking slow and carrying something in one of her hands. When she sat back down on the curb beside them, she was silent for a long time until finally Glenda asked her what she had seen.

Nadine finally responded that she had entered the building and climbed slowly to the second floor landing. She confirmed to herself, and to her friends, that it would have been impossible, had the chair been sitting on the landing, for them to have missed seeing the chair sitting on the landing when they had earlier climbed to the third floor.

Nadine continued that when she went back inside the building by herself she had slowly climbed the stairs to the second floor landing. The chair was still

---

[113] This photo is from the author's collection.

sitting where they had left it in the center of the small landing. It was impossible for them to have missed seeing the chair if it had been present as they had climbed the stairs the first time.

Figure 34: This is a photo taken by Edward Weissbard and given to the El Paso Times. It shows a figure in the lower left hand window of the building.

Nadine paused and then continued relating her story. She said that she had continued up the stairs to the third floor, looking to see if perhaps another person had somehow gotten inside the building and was playing a trick on the three of them. The third floor was silent and dark just as it had been when they had gotten to the third floor earlier. Finally, satisfied, Nadine turned and descended the stairs to the second floor landing. As she glanced at the chair she had earlier examined in detail, she froze, her blood running cold. There, lying on the seat of the chair was a large handle like from a gate.

Nadine held the large handle up for her friends to see. The dim street lights reflecting from the dull metal of the item in her hand. They all agreed the handle had not been sitting on the seat of the chair as the three of them had descended the stairs earlier, and Nadine swore that it had not been on the seat of the chair as she had examined the chair closely in her solo trip to the third floor. So how had it gotten there? The three of them never arrived at an answer.

As the three of them sat on the curb discussing the mysteries of the evening, a Military Police officer came by and asked them to identify themselves. He relaxed when Glenda Bromberg identified herself as the wife of BG Bromberg, but he stressed several times that they should not trespass inside of Building 4. All three of the women, the events from their impromptu ghost hunt fresh in their minds assured the MP that they would not enter the building without permission. As they talked the MP began to talk about some of the stories he had both heard about as well as some incidents that he had experienced himself inside of Building 4. Surprisingly, he made mention of the chair that seemed to move about the building that they had just dealt with. He also mentioned that on occasion patrol dogs refused to enter the building.

Glenda asked if the MP could take them through the Building about which they had heard so much, but he told them he had to get permission to do so and he did not think permission would be granted. She asked if he would at least ask and he left to return to the MP station. In a few minutes he returned with a large flashlight and told them that permission had been granted. Taking a deep breath, he led them into the most haunted building on Fort Bliss.

She mentioned that the MP was a very big man, but she could tell that he was very shaky entering Building 4 after dark. As they walked around the dark, silent building, he regaled them with stories of events that had been reported in the building.

The day that I took the photos of Katelyn Hobson, the daughter of Colonel and Mrs. Hobson[114] and Glenda Bromberg at Building 4, we took another impromptu tour. To my surprise, the doors were open, the boards of the doors at the front of the building were gone and the doors were standing open. This time, rather than smelling cinnamon or some other odd odor, as I entered each empty cluttered office I suddenly began to feel as if I was intruding into an area that was, or should be, off limits to all of us. There was no one I could see inside the building except the three of us, but I had the distinct impression that I was disturbing someone or something that was not happy with my presence. Putting the feeling in the back of my mind, I proceeded to take a large number of photos of my two volunteer models such as the ones on the next few pages.

---

[114] Katelyn Hobson is a rising country music star.

Figure 35: Notice that the floor seems remarkably clean for a building that has been boarded up for years.

CHAPTER NINE
BUILDING 8

Figure 36: Building 8 as it looks today.

Building 8 was built in 1893 as the first hospital for Fort Bliss and contained 4,845 square feet. The rectangular building was constructed in Greek Revival style with a limestone foundation, brick water table and walls. The frieze band is embellished with a brick dogtooth course, brick stretchers and headers, wood moldings and metal cavetto molding. The building was originally painted a cream color.

The structure has a medium pitched hipped roof and symmetrically placed windows are double hung wood sash with 2/2 lights and screens. The original design called for a two story Stick Style porch with a shed roof that encircled the entire building[115].

It served this function until 1916 when Building 1 assumed that role on the growing Post[116]. The original design of the Building included porticos to provide shade from the hot Texas sun in those days before air conditioning. There was also originally a ramp or walkway that connected Building 8 to Building 9 to enable gurneys to be easily rolled from the Hospital to the Morgue. This walkway is a thing of the post.

Figure 37: A picture of Building 8 as it was originally designed, courtesy of Heidi Crabtree

---

[115] National Register of Historic Places Registration Form for the Fort Bliss Main Post Historic District, 2nd Edition, November 2000.
[116] Crabtree, Heidi Veronica, An Overview of the Histories and Myths of Fort Bliss' Oldest Buildings, A Crabtree Hollow Book, 2000.

According to the stories I have heard, Building 8 also has presences that are more sensed rather than seen. The sounds of footsteps are heard when no one else is around as well as the occasional sound of whispering.

CHAPTER TEN
BUILDING 9

Figure 38: Building 9, the original morgue at Fort Bliss.

Building 9 is a two story Greek Revival style building that was constructed in 1893 to serve at the original morgue and contains 968 square feet and was originally designated as Building 54. This building is constructed with a limestone foundation, brick watertable and walls, and has been painted cream. The frieze band is embellished with a brick dogtooth course, brick stretchers and headers, wood moldings and metal cavetto moldings.

The building has a medium pitched hipped roof. The symmetrically placed windows are double hung wood sash with 2/2 lights and screens. The building originally had a one-story Stick Style porch with shed roof that encircled the entire building.

When this building was no longer needed for its original purpose, in typical Army fashion, the structure was turned to another use. Rather than tear the building down, the former morgue became a conference room. Where once surgeons conducted autopsies and drained bodily fluids into drains that still exist beneath the tiles that now cover the floor, administrators now sat at their ease considering issues less life and death than those the building was designed to address.

But does this mean that the spirits of those whose earthly remains passed through the doors of this once bustling morgue have gone to the next world? No not at all. In fact, according to Connie Wang, psychic and my co-author in this series, many people report feeling uncomfortable while inside the walls of this building. She told me that at one time, this building housed a computer center. There was a lot of trouble with the equipment as computers and other electrical devices would switch on and off without any human hands touching them.

Her belief and my own as well, is that the spirits of some of those whose last port of call was inside this small building simply have not left.

CHAPTER ELEVEN
BUILDING 12

Building 12 is a two story building built in 1915 as a barracks for enlisted men, containing 10,511 square feet. According to Heidi Crabtree, this building was originally designated as Building 226[117]. This nondescript rectangular building was constructed with a poured concrete foundation, brick walls and a brick belt course above the second floor windows. The building is covered with a medium double-pitched hipped roof. The original open two story full width porch located on the west side of the building has been enclosed with brick to provide additional usable space inside the building. Double-hung wood sash windows with 6/6 lighting and screen are used throughout the building.

The building has served many different roles for the military to include a rather exciting past as it once served as the Office of Special Weapons, as nuclear weapons were once referred to. Then the name was changed to the Institute of Nuclear Studies and later the U.S. Army Nuclear Agency before that entity was transferred to Fort Belvoir, MD.

More than one individual has reported seeing someone standing looking out an upper window in this building, when the building has been empty and secured for the night. Heidi Crabtree in her short book makes reference to a

---

[117] Crabtree, Heidi Veronica, An Overview of the Histories and Myths of Fort Bliss' Oldest Buildings, A Crabtree Hollow Book, 2000.

civilian employee working in Building 12 who locked up the building and went to her car only to see someone[118] looking out of an upper window. She was very certain she had locked the building securely.

An immediate search by quickly summoned military police failed to find that anyone had been in the building.

.

---

[118] The figure looked like a man.

CHAPTER TWELVE
BUILDING 13

Figure 39: Building 13 as originally built[119].

---

[119] Photo courtesy of Susan Payne, Archivist, Fort Bliss Directorate of Environment.

The three story building designated as Building 13 was built in 1893 as a troop barracks in accordance with the Quartermaster General standard plan with simplified Queen Anne or Folk Victorian style elements. The original structure contained 27,553 square feet. According to Heidi Crabtree the original designation was as Building number 59. The C-shaped building is constructed with a brick foundation and yellow brick walls. The building was constructed with a three-story center section flanked by two story wings. The center section has a double pitched hipped roof with gable dormers with decorative unglazed terra cotta. The wings have double pitched hipped roofs with shed roof dormers.

The two story additions were constructed n the ear, or east, side of the building's flanking wings with red brick. The additions were constructed with double pitched gable roofs. The end walls have triple corbelled chimney piers below the roof line. The building's original two story wood porches were removed and new concrete porches with pipe columns and railing were added in their places. The building is equipped with double-hung wood sash windows with 4/4 lighting and also contains quarter-round windows set within the gables[120].

Over the years it had many uses, first as a barracks for enlisted men and then later as administrative offices. In 1968 half of the building was used for administrative activities and half of it was used as a Post Exchange[121]. It currently houses the Staff Judge Advocate Staff, the Army CID and a military courtroom.

A large number of stories have come from this stately old building. According to Heidi Crabtree, an officer working in Building 13 told her that he had been working late one evening and suddenly heard loud banging coming from the door leading to the attic storeroom. At that moment, there was no doubt in his mind that someone was locked inside the attic. He cautiously opened the door and found – nothing. The attic storeroom was completely empty. There was no explanation for the banging that he had heard. He decided it was time for him to go home for the day.

Connie Wang believes that there are restless spirits that inhabit that old building, destined never to find rest until vindicated. Perhaps this is true and perhaps it is not, but it is an interesting thought.

---

[120] National Register of Historic Places Registration Form for the Fort Bliss Main Post Historic District, 2nd Edition, November 2000.
[121] Crabtree, Heidi Veronica, An Overview of the Histories and Myths of Fort Bliss' Oldest Buildings, A Crabtree Hollow Book, 2000.

Figure 40: Interior view of Building 13[122].

When I took the Fort Bliss Ghost Tour given by Colonel (P) Lennox, he told us of stories of the doors to the Courtroom swinging open and closed by themselves. Individuals who have worked late and know that they are the last ones to leave the building, get to their cars and turn back to see windows open and lights burning as if others are still inside the building. Windows are open, I might add, they are very certain that they closed prior to leaving the building and lights are on that these witnesses were sure were not burning when they walked out of the silent building.

Others have told of ghostly soldiers being seen walking in the hallways. According to one of Colonel (P) Lennox's sons, from his bedroom he could see the front of Building 13 and regularly saw lights and moving figures in the upper windows of the building.

There has been much talk about a suicide that supposedly took place in the attic of Building 13. In this attic, which is a scene of much spooky activity if witnesses are to be believed, a soldier, dejected over being forced to leave the Army hung himself with a piece of wire.

Research into this alleged suicide reveals that in the El Pastimes[123] there is a story of a soldier by the name of Carl Schiller, a member of Company M,

---

[122] Photo courtesy of Susan Payne, Archivist, Fort Bliss Directorate of Environment.

309th Infantry who had been sent o Fort Bliss for discharge. Only a few hours before he was to be mustered out, Schiller's body was found hanging in an "unoccupied building" about 8:00 am. He had supposedly hung himself with a length of wire. Heidi Crabtree believed that he had hung himself in the attic of Building 13 and everything that I can find out about this death also leads me to believe the same thing[124].

However, I am not of the opinion that this man's death was a suicide. In fact, all of the evidence seems to point to the fact that he was not depressed nor had he expressed any regrets at leaving the service. So why would he hang himself?

According to the article, a Court of Inquiry composed of Military Officers, individuals who might be counted upon to return a verdict that would lessen the embarrassment felt by the Army at such an unexplained death, were unable to find a motive for Schiller's death and so returned a verdict of suicide. However, the available evidence would seem to make suicide a somewhat implausible decision. Schiller's comrades all testified that he had been in good spirits the night before and all other evidence made it clear that Schiller was in good health and good spirits since arriving at Fort Bliss.

On the day of his death, June 11, 1919, he arose at 7:00 am with the other men, had a quiet breakfast and made no unusual actions or comments that anyone could remember. He was then supposed to have taken his own life at about 8:00 am and the body was found at around 10:00 am

As a result of the decision of the Board of Inquiry, no true investigation into a possible murder was ever conducted, but being murdered in such a grisly manner would certainly account for a ghostly presence in this building. Also ask yourself, if the building was unoccupied as stated in the article, why were others in the building and most importantly, why did they feel a need to enter the attic of an "unoccupied" building? Unfortunately, these questions will never be answered.

[123] El Paso Times, *Arizona Soldier Hangs Self With Wire At Bliss*, June 12, 1919.
[124] Crabtree, Heidi Veronica, <u>An Overview of the Histories and Myths of Fort Bliss' Oldest Buildings</u>, A Crabtree Hollow Book, 2000

CHAPTER THIRTEEN
BUILDING 54

Building 54 was built in 1919, and contains 8,897 square feet. Heidi Crabtree has written that this building was originally designated as Building 401[125]. The L-shaped building, with a basement, is constructed with a concrete foundation, brick walls and a medium pitched, kicked eave hipped roof. There is a large brick four-story tower located at the building's southwest corner that is used to dry the fire hoses. The tower has a low-pitched hipped roof and louvered openings on all four sides to provide ventilation. The building contains center-pivot steel window and double-hung wood sash windows. The center pivot windows located in the second floor sleeping area are equipped with projecting wedge-shaped screens that allow sashes to operate. The building contains three segmented overhead doors on the west elevation and two segmented overhead doors on the east elevation[126]. Today, this building still serves the same purpose as when it was built so many years ago, it is the home of the Fort Bliss Fire Department.

According to some of the stories told about this building, reflections of an individual can be seen in a particular mirror when no one has been standing in front of the mirror. More than one individual has said that he can sit in the dispatcher's office and watch someone roaming around at night. However, when attempts are made to identify the individual seen roaming around, no one can be found.

---

[125] Crabtree, Heidi Veronica, An Overview of the Histories and Myths of Fort Bliss' Oldest Buildings, A Crabtree Hollow Book, 2000
[126]National Register of Historic Places Registration Form for the Fort Bliss Main Post Historic District, 2nd Edition, November 2000.

As with most firehouses, there are beds upstairs for the firemen on duty. In this area apparitions have been seen by more than one fireman coming up to catch a quick nap and the security cameras have also caught glimpses of figures in this area when all of the firemen have been elsewhere. One fireman who did doze off reported that he woke up to see someone standing over the bed.

During the Great Fort Bliss Ghost Tour hosted by Colonel (P) Lennox, these and other stories about this particular building were told to us, though, unfortunately, we were not allowed to enter the firehouse. However, we did see some lights that seemed not to have a rational explanation.

CHAPTER FOURTEEN
BUILDING 117

The two story building that is designated as Building 117 was built in 1915 as a troop barracks and contains 9,351 square feet. This nondescript rectangular building was constructed with a poured concrete foundation, brick walls and a brick belt course above the second floor windows. The building is covered with a medium double-pitched hipped roof. An open two story full width porch located on the west side of the building and included under the building's hipped roof. Double-hung wood sash windows with 6/6 lighting and screen are used throughout the building[127].

Those originally a troop billet, its current use is to house the administrative sections of the 76th Military Police Battalion (PROV) and Military Intelligence. As an administrative facility, when the duty day is ended, this building is secured and no one remains after the duty day. The operational element of the 76th Military Police Battalion (PROV) is stationed in Building 116, along with Physical Security and the Provost Marshall's Office[128].

From the various stories that I have heard, there is definitely something going on inside of Building 117 when the lights go out. Since all administrative support functions for the MP station were conducted in Building 117 and the Army hates duplication of effort or equipment, after duty hours, if MPs on duty

---

[127] National Register of Historic Places Registration Form for the Fort Bliss Main Post Historic District, 2nd Edition, November 2000.

[128] Crabtree, Heidi Veronica, An Overview of the Histories and Myths of Fort Bliss' Oldest Buildings, A Crabtree Hollow Book, 2000.

needed to make copies they had to go across the Building 117 to use the copiers in the closed administrative section.

A large number of people who have had occasion to need to make copies in Building 117 after duty hours, have maintained that at night the sounds of doors opening and closing and people walking on the second floor can be clearly heard.

There is a story that was told by one Military Policeman[129] that seems to be fairly representative of what happens to those unwise enough or unlucky enough to have to go into this building late at night to make copies[130].

He had entered the building through the rear door that faces the MP station and was preparing to make his copies when he heard the front door open and close as if someone had entered. Believing that it was one of his colleagues coming to make copies, he walked from the copy room to the hallway where he could see the front door. He saw no one in the corridor. He then went and checked the door and it was firmly secured, needing a key to unlock it. Not really knowing what to think, he returned to the copy room and almost immediately began to hear someone walking back and forth in the room directly over where he was making the copies.

Even though he was positive that there was no one else in the building, he felt that he had to check out what was making the sounds that he could so clearly hear. Cautiously, he unlocked the front door and using the outside stairs climbed to the second floor veranda. He looked in one of the windows, but was unable to see anyone moving about inside the locked building. Deciding to finish his copying job, he returned to the first floor and found that the front door that he had unlocked and left unlocked while he went to the second floor was now securely locked. Even though it takes a key to either lock or unlock the door, somehow, in the few minutes he had been upstairs, someone or something had locked the door.

Deciding that enough was enough, he returned to the MP station minus his copies and made the Desk Sergeant go get the copies that he had left inside Building 117. He refused to go back into the building. It was also referenced in another email in my possession that several of the ladies that worked on the MP Desk[131] would not enter Building 117 for any reason.

It would seem that this spirit or spirits is/are content to allow the Army to possess the building during daylight hours, but the night belongs to him (or them).

---

[129] I have a copy of the e-mail that he sent to Heidi Crabtree that very clearly describes what happened to him, but since she chose not to use his name, neither will I.
[130] A version of this story is to be found in: Crabtree, Heidi Veronica, An Overview of the Histories and Myths of Fort Bliss' Oldest Buildings, A Crabtree Hollow Book, 2000
[131] Blotter clerks.

CHAPTER FIFTEEN
PERSHING HOUSE

The house located at 228 Sheridan Road, Fort Bliss, Texas has had many different names since its construction, such as Quarters Number One, Quarters 228, the Commanding General's Quarters and now, finally, The Pershing House[132]. The designation 'The Pershing House' was applied to his historic old structure after it was occupied by General Pershing in the early 1900s.

Construction on this grand old home was in keeping with the requirements of 'Army Plan Number 243, Field Officer's Quarters: two stories, full basement." The architecture is a combination of Georgian Revival and Plantation style, with the end result being reminiscent of the antebellum plantation homes found in Louisiana.

The two-story building was constructed in 1910 at a cost of $16,000.00 and contains 5,874 square feet. Other existing quarters of this type can still be found at Fort Sam Houston, Texas and Fort Sill, Oklahoma[133]. The irregular plan building is constructed with a reinforced concrete foundation, watertable, running bond painted (white) yellow brick walls, and a low pitched hipped roof with exposed rater ends and one chimney. The building contains a partial basement and a crawlspace.

---

[132] Author unknown, <u>The Pershing House, Fort Bliss, Texas</u>, a power point presentation from the Fort Bliss website.
[133] Ibid

GENERAL OF THE ARMIES
JOHN JOSEPH PERSHING 1860-1948

There is a two-tier verandah that is supported by eleven green painted wood columns per level. The main entrance to the home, originally contained double doors centered on the east elevation, but this has been altered to consist of a wood panel door with elliptical fanlight and exterior screen door. Secondary single wood panel doors are located on the south, west and north elevations. Double hung wood windows with 2/2 lighting are used throughout the home. The lintels are arched brick and the sills are concrete[134].

The original floor plan had a central hallway, flanked on the let by a parlor and adjoining library and on the right by a dining room and pantry toward the rear of the house. The original design called for large corner fireplaces in each of the formal front rooms, but the fireplaces as well as the chimneys have been removed in one of the later renovations of the home. An open passageway separated the kitchen and staff quarters at the rear of the home from the rest of the first floor[135].

The original design of the upstairs family quarters called for four large bedrooms and three smaller ones. These seven bedrooms on the upper level combined with the two staff bedrooms downstairs, gave the residence nine bedrooms all told. The original plumbing design included two bathrooms upstairs in the family quarters and one bathroom downstairs in the staff quarters.

In the full basement were the boiler room that furnished the heating, the laundry room as well as a storage area. The original lighting for the home was furnished by kerosene lamps until 1911 when the somewhat dangerous lamps were replaced by electric lights. Meals were prepared on old fashioned cook stoves until 1928, when natural gas was added for both cooking and heating.

Over the years, the 4,697 square foot home has been remodeled a number of times. The original seven bedrooms on the second floor have been reduced to five. The laundry room has been moved from the basement to the first floor and now it is located in the rear of the second floor.

---

[134] National Register of Historic Places Registration Form for the Fort Bliss Main Post Historic District, 2nd Edition, November 2000.
[135] Author unknown, The Pershing House, Fort Bliss, Texas, a power point presentation from the Fort Bliss website.

From its completion in 1910, until 1934 when the Shipton House was

Figure 41: The Pershing House Today

completed as the new commanding general's quarters, The Pershing House served as the official residence of the senior commanders of Fort Bliss. Currently, it serves as the residence of the Deputy Commanding General.

Guests who have stayed at the Pershing House include Mexican General Victoriano Huerta, future President of Mexico; William F. "Buffalo Bill" Cody and, of all people, Pancho Villa, who stayed a short time at the residence as a guest of General Pershing[136].

General Pershing was stationed at Fort Bliss and occupied these quarters from April of 1914 until he left for Fort Sam Houston to become Commander of the Southern District in February 1917. Though he was the senior officer stationed at Fort Bliss during this time period, he was not the Post Commander. During this time period Fort Bliss was commanded by Colonel George H. Morgan from May 1914 until April 1915 and then again from May 1915 until September 1915. Colonel Franklin O. Johnson commanded the Post from April to May 1915; Colonel Charles W. Taylor commanded from September 1915 until October 1916 and Colonel John W. Heard commanded from October to December 1916[137].

---

[136] Ibid
[137] Ibid

Figure 42: General Pershing and Pancho Villa

General Pershing had been stationed at the Presidio in San Francisco, CA and commanded the 8th Infantry Brigade on detached service from the Presidio and after Pancho Villa's raid on Columbus, New Mexico, he commanded the Punitive Expedition that pursued Villa into Mexico from March 15, 1916 until February 5, 1917. He had traveled to Fort Bliss unaccompanied; leave his wife and 5 children at the Presidio. On August 15, 1915, General Pershing received word that his wife and 4 of his children had died of smoke inhalation in a fire that broke out in their quarters at the Presidio. It was from this tragic event that his personality seemed to change and he became known as a cold withdrawn individual[138]. There are those who believe that General Pershing, himself, is one of the spirits that haunt this grand old home. He had thought to enjoy it with his family, to whom he was devoted, but instead, it was here that he received the bad news. Perhaps he does haunt the scene of this devastating news.

With such a distinguished history and so much sadness taking place within its walls, there is no wonder that the home known as 'The Pershing House" has uninvited and invisible occupants.

I had occasion to have a long talk with Glenda Bromberg, wife of Brigadier General Howard Bromberg, Commander of the 32nd Army Air and Missile Defense Command and the current occupants of The Pershing House.

---

[138] Ibid

She had several stories to tell about her interactions with the unseen in the house she and her family had come to love.

Glenda Bromberg[139] had been one of those that guided the Great Fort Bliss Ghost Tour that Colonel (P) Lennox and his family had put on for us. Her knowledge of the history and mystery of Fort Bliss covers many diverse areas and her assistance in preparing this book has been invaluable. One afternoon, she and her husband, only recently returned from the Middle East took time from their busy schedule to sit with me and relate some of the stories they had to tell about The Pershing House.

According to Glenda, one afternoon in January 2000, two friends came over to The Pershing House with a bottle of champagne. The intention of the friends was to toast the New Year with General Bromberg and his wife. Though it was the middle of the day, the four individuals had adjourned to the living room to enjoy the champagne. Four glasses were poured and General Bromberg asked his wife if he should light the three small candles that sat on the glass covered wicker coffee table.

Figure 43: The wicker coffee table where the candles moved.

At his wife's agreement, the General lit the 3 candles and as he lit the third one, one of the glasses of champagne moved approximately 5 inches.

---

[139] At the risk of being considered overly familiar, and with the greatest of respect, from here on out, I will refer to Mrs. Bromberg as Glenda.

Glenda said that there was no sound and the liquid in the glass never moved. There was no condensation on the glass table top and no reason that they could find for the glass to have moved.

Glenda told me that her family had moved into The Pershing House in July of 2000 and then almost immediately they had to make a trip. Since they had a dog and two cats, she had not wanted to either put the animals into a kennel or leave them in the house alone. The then Commanding General's Aide de Camp, Captain Jan Icoff had volunteered to stay at The Pershing House for the two weeks that the Brombergs would be gone and care for the animals. Captain Icoff was a serious, no nonsense officer, no afraid to stay in a large old home by herself.

Figure 44: Buffalo Bill Cody and BG Hugh Scott in front of the Pershing House[140].

According to what Captain Icoff told Glenda, she had a most interesting stay for the short time that she occupied the old home. According to the story, she would arrive at her temporary home each evening to find lights on the second floor burning brightly, though she was certain that she had made sure that all lights were turned off prior to leaving for work. She decided that since the house was old, perhaps the switches were not functioning properly.

One night, the Captain was awakened by the sounds of someone clanging pots and pans in the kitchen as if preparing to cook a meal. She later told Glenda that she decided that she had only two courses of action at that point. She could, she said, simply lie in the bed until whatever or whoever, it was making the sounds went away or she could go investigate. Finally, she decided to investigate.

---

[140] Photo from author's collection.

According to Glenda Bromberg, when the Captain entered the kitchen, it was ice cold to the point that she could see her breath. Finding no one, visible that is, she returned to bed.

The next day the Captain arrived at The Pershing House planning to do her laundry. She had carefully packed all of her dirty clothing into a basket that she had placed in the corner of the bedroom she was occupying. When she arrived 'home' that day, she found the basket of dirty clothing sitting in the middle of the floor in her bedroom. At that point, she decided it was time to leave, so she took the dog and both cats and returned to her own quarters until the Brombergs returned to the Post.

Glenda said that all of her family had heard various noises that could not be explained. Her oldest daughter, Leah complained that she had trouble sleeping because she would hear the sounds of rocking as if someone was sitting in a rocking chair in her room, slowly rocking back and forth. It is interesting to note that a short time later, a friend to Glenda that they had driven past the house one afternoon and noticed a woman in a blue dress sitting in a rocking chair on one of the wide verandas upstairs. In keeping with the Plantation style of the house, both upstairs and down there are wide verandas on both levels.

Jennifer, the second daughter told her mother that several times she had heard her name whispered when there was no one else around and on several nights as she had been drifting off to sleep, she had felt a gentle hand softly caress her cheek when there had been no one else in her bedroom.

Glenda also said that periodically when they would enter the house they would be surrounded by strange odors. She could not really explain what type of odors she was referring to; she could only describe it as smelling old.

One night, she entered the kitchen to find the dog, Sandy standing silently starring fixedly at the sink area as if he was watching something or someone standing at that location. Glenda could not detect anything wrong, as the dog was not acting upset or tense, but when she went to walk over toward the sink, the dog immediately blocked the way and would not let her pass. She never had any indication what had been in her kitchen, but the dog acted to protect her in the only way that he could, by keeping her away from what he clearly felt was danger.

She also told me of a former Commanding General's Aide de Camp, she could not give me any more specific information as to date, time or the name of the aide, who had responded to a complaint that the sprinklers at the Pershing House were running. The Aide had gone over and cut the sprinklers off, but one older looking sprinkler continued to run, totally unaffected by his shutting off the water. Believing that the sprinkler was defective, the Aide turned in a work order to have the faulty sprinkler repaired. Imagine everyone's surprise when the workers who dug up the water line found that the sprinkler that refused to shut off was not even connected to a water line. There was no possible way that this particular sprinkler could have worked, but a large number of witnesses confirmed that this sprinkler had been happily spraying water across the green lawn[141].

Glenda also told me about waking up at about 2:00 in the morning and smelling coffee brewing and bacon frying when there was no one in the kitchen. She said that no one in her household was a heavy coffee drinker and so they did not have a coffee maker set on a timer. She also said that the neighbors were too far away for the smell to be coming from their houses and few, if any, of them would be brewing coffee at that hour of the morning.

Her last story had to do with another smell that she has often smelled in the evening after the children have gone to bed. As she sits in her den, she can often detect the smell of cigarette smoke as if someone in the house was smoking. She said that no one in her family, or as far as she knows on the street, smokes. However, if does fit in with her feeling that one of the spirits in the house is female. Since smoking by females was taboo for so many years, she has the impression of a woman finally getting her children to bed and then taking time out for a forbidden smoke before going to bed. It makes her feel a little closer to the spirit, who she seems to firmly believe, is friendly.

The last story of the spirits at The Pershing House again came from the website called Haunted Fort Bliss[142], though this story has been related to me by several others familiar with the ghostly history of this historic old Post.

According to this story, it seems that there was a dinner that took place at the Pershing House in the 1980s. This dinner was a gathering of senior officers and one of the senior officers present was Afro-American. This officer, I have been told that he was a Lieutenant Colonel, asked the officer next to him to please pass him the salt. As his neighbor obligingly reached for the salt shaker, everyone was shocked to see the shaker rise into the air, float past the one who had asked for it and land upright in front of the officer seated next to him. Are spirits prejudiced? Many years ago, though Black soldiers served with distinction and Black officers were not uncommon, there was still a certain prejudice from those at higher levels.

This prejudice was still strong even in the 1970s and 1980s that even as a Second Lieutenant in an Infantry Battalion, I was very much aware of this feeling from the Battalion and Brigade staffs. Was one of the spirits in the Pershing House making its prejudice against Black officers known?

There individual who posts the information on Haunted Fort Bliss is also a friend of the Brombergs. According to the section on The Pershing House, this individual was at the house helping Glenda Bromberg decorate for a Halloween Party. It is reported that the author of the website[143], Glenda Bromberg and her

---

[141] This particular story can also be found at a website called Haunted Fort Bliss. This site can be found at http://www.angelfire.com/tx4/bustersbattery/haunted.html

[142] Ibid

[143] Though the author does not make his or her identity known on the site, it is clearly Heidi Crabtree, who completed the first serious investigation into some of the stories associated with Fort Bliss.

daughters all caught a whiff of potato peeling in the kitchen area. Though this smell was described as very strong, there were no potato peelings anywhere in the kitchen[144]. Perhaps the ghost was going to prepare some potatoes to go with the bacon and coffee that are so often smelled.

---

[144] Ibid

CHAPTER SIXTEEN
WILLIAM BEAUMONT ARMY MEDICAL CENTER

The William Beaumont General Hospital was one of the U.S. Army's five original general hospitals. It opened at fort Bliss on July 1, 1921 although the facility was not actually completed until the following year. The hospital originally consisted of forty-eight tile and stucco buildings with a bed capacity of approximately 414 patients. The staff consisted of six officers, two nurses and thirty enlisted men. William Beaumont General Hospital's original mission was to provide general medical care to border patrol troops stationed at Fort Bliss. By the 1930s, however, the hospital was serving the entire western portion of the Army's Eighth Corps area, providing healthcare to soldiers stationed at posts in Arizona, New Mexico and western Texas[145].

When Congress authorized a limited peacetime mobilization just prior to the nation's entry into World War II, the Army initiated a major expansion program at William Beaumont General Hospital to increase its ability to handle the medical needs of the greatly expanded Army. During the World War II era, the hospital received new wards, instructional buildings, quarters, storehouses, repair shops and recreational facilities. This new construction pushed the total

---

[145] Inventory & Evaluation of the Historic William Beaumont General Hospital Area at the William Beaumont Army Medical Center at fort Bliss, Texas by Tri-Services Cultural Resources Research Lab. This short history was given to me courtesy of Susan Payne, Archivist, Fort Bliss Directorate of Environment.

number of buildings at the hospital to 174 and the number of available beds to nearly 6,000. During the World War II, the William Beaumont General Hospital trained approximately 16,000 medical technicians, including over 1,000 WAC[146] recruits. The hospital also became a specialty center for plastic surgery, ophthalmic surgery, neuropsychiatry ad deep radiation therapy. In the last year of the war alone, some 26,358 patients received medical treatment at William Beaumont.

The William Beaumont Army Medical Center, at Fort Bliss, was known as William Beaumont General Hospital when it opened on July 1, 1921. At that time the hospital, constructed at a cost of $1.6 million, consisted of thirty-seven buildings and had a normal bed capacity of 403. The hospital was on a 120-acre tract just west of Fort Bliss and served as the post hospital. After the construction of a new base hospital, it continued to serve Fort Bliss for special cases and also served Biggs Field, Fort Huachuca, Fort D. A. Russell, Luke Field, the Tucson Air Base, Camp Barkeley, and Albuquerque Air Base.

By 1937 the hospital had been expanded to seventy buildings, and in 1941 it opened a School for Medical Department Technicians. During World War II the hospital received particular recognition for its work in plastic surgery. The hospital was named for William Beaumont, a nineteenth century army physician who pioneered the study of the human digestive process. A new $17.5 million, twelve-story building was dedicated on July 1, 1972, and in 1973, when it became a teaching hospital, the name of the facility was changed to William Beaumont Army Medical Center. The three-story Bradley Building, named for Gen. Omar Bradley, was added in 1982. William Beaumont Army Medical Center has a capacity of 600 beds; employs 1,500 military and 700 civilian personnel; and serves all of West Texas, New Mexico, Arizona, and part of southern California. It has one of only two trauma units in the El Paso area.

William Beaumont General Hospital was one of only ten, of the Army's sixty-three, general hospitals retained after World War II. Besides providing medical care to returning wounded soldiers during both the Korea War and the police action in Vietnam, the hospital also provided general medicine and surgical services to veterans and personnel at Fort Bliss and other regional military installations. By the mid-1060s, the needs of the Army began to surpass the capabilities of the hospital. Consequently, the Army constructed a new, modern, twelve story facility to the west of the existing hospital. This new state of the art facility, known as the William Beaumont Army Medical Center, opened in 1972 and became the Southwest's major regional Army Medical Center.

As the mission of Beaumont changed, some of the older buildings were used for different purposes. Some of them became administrative buildings which were staffed by civilian personnel in support of military personnel. Connie Wang told me about one female civilian supervisor who was working late one

---

[146] Women's Army Corp

evening an looked up to see a woman standing in her doorway. The visitor had appeared without a sound and just stood silently staring at the startled worker.

The worker described her visitor as a good looking, blonde blue-eyed woman wearing a starched white nurse's uniform. The insignia on the uniform identified the woman as a member of the Women's Army Corp. For a long time, the two just stared at each other before the woman in white faded away. The employee got her things and went home as quickly as possible.

I also have another email that was sent to Heidi Crabtree from an MP who had been assigned to Fort Bliss with the 76th MP BN (PROV). His wife was also an MP and periodically patrolled the William Beaumont area. According to the email, his wife saw her ghost in one of the buildings adjacent to William Beaumont Army Medical Center.

According to the story related in the email, the email author's wife was on a midnight shift and patrolling the area around the old hospital. There had been a lot of reports about people sneaking into the old buildings and using drugs, so a system of routine checks of the buildings had been ordered.

On the evening in question, as she drove past the old buildings, she distinctly saw the figure of a man standing in one of the upper windows. She stopped the car and kept looking at the figure, which was clearly visible in the upper window. After about a minute or so the figure slowly faded away. A later search of this building revealed so sign that anyone had been in the building.

Figure 45: Map showing the Physical evolution of William Beaumont General Hospital from 1920 to 1945.

CHAPTER SEVENTEEN
OFFICERS ROW IN
FRONT OF THE OFFICERS CLUB

I was never stationed at Fort Bliss, since it has long been the home of the Artillery and I was commissioned as an Infantry Officer[147]. After being sent to play in the jungle in several interesting countries, I spent my CONUS time at Fort Benning, the home of the Infantry. However, one thing that hunting and being hunted in the jungle in a foreign land does for those who survive it, is give you the ability to sense when something is not exactly as it should be.

Since obtaining a membership in the Fort Bliss Officers Club, I have always wondered why, when I get out of my car and start for the entrance of the Club, I get a strange feeling as if something is not quite as it should be. I am retired and not being hunted nor am I hunting anyone or anything unless you count the ghosts of this historic old post, but perhaps this next story could be a partial explanation for my feeling. We all but follow in the footsteps of those who came before and perhaps they leave emotions as well as possessions behind them.

The Officers Club sits atop a hill overlooking what was the Fort Bliss Polo Field. The Club Building has been in use for many years and a lot of activity once took place around the Polo Field.

---

[147] In all seriousness, my first Battalion Commander (Infantry, naturally) once told me that Artillery Officers were a necessary evil, but you certainly wouldn't want your daughter to marry one.

I have in my possession a copy of an email sent to Heidi Crabtree by a member of the Military Police[148]. In this email, he discussed an event that took place on the road that runs behind officers' row and in front of the Officers Club. I would one day like to be able to determine what led to this haunting, for it could explain much.

According to the author of the email, in the summer of 1996, the 978th Military Police Company was deployed and the soldiers of the Center Military Police Company were working 12 hour shifts. The author was working the midnight shift. He wrote that about 0200 (2 am for you civilians) a call was received from an individual living in front of the Officers Club[149].

The caller reported that she had heard a noise outside her home and saw a girl in her back yard. The girl was wearing a blue dress and was just walking around as if looking for someone or something. The caller reported that the little girl looked to be about 8 – 10 years old.

The author or the email said that they (two patrols) immediately responded to the call and when they entered the back yard, they saw the little girl, though by this time she was out of the back yard and walking in the road directly in front of the Officers Club. The author's Military Police partner called for the little girl to stop and wait for them, that they were police as soon as he saw her, but though she did turn and look at them, the little girl continued to walk down the street toward Pershing Gate.

The author and his partner broke into a slow jog after the girl and saw the little girl turn onto the street that leads directly to Pershing Gate. As the two MPs rounded the corner after the girl, they saw her turn and walk through the fence line and down the hill toward the old Polo Field. Needless to say, they were dumbfounded because there were no holes in that fence line, the girl had walked through a barrier that should have stopped her dead in her tracks. The little girl seemed to vanish as she reached the Polo Field[150]. Where did she come from and where did she go? No one was ever able to answer those questions.

As a final entry on this story, not wanting to admit that they had brushed up against the unknown, the two MPs reported to the Desk Sergeant that they had returned to little girl to her parents. That is also the story that they told to the originally caller when she called to make sure they had found the little girl.

Where did she come from and what was she looking for? Those answers are lost in the mists of time. I am curious as to how the little girl, who is always described as walking, was able to outdistance two physically fit, jogging Military Policemen.

---

[148] In her writings she chose not to name the individual who sent her this story and those I have had no such request, I will follow her lead in not naming the source of this story.

[149] The houses in front of the Officers Club is called Officers Row, field grade housing that includes The Pershing House.

[150] The Polo Field in question was undoubtedly Armstrong Field, named for Lieutenant Eugene Victor Armstrong, who was killed in a polo accident at the field in 1914.

CHAPTER EIGHTEEN
FORT BLISS CEMETERY

The Fort Bliss Cemetery is a plot of land that is hallowed by the deaths of so many young men and women in service to their country. With so many who

Figure 46: Fort Bliss Cemetery at night taken with an infra-red filter.

suffered and dead in service confined into this one area, it is little wonder that from time to time, some spirits may become restless and try to associate with the living.

This story comes from an email sent to Heidi Crabtree that I was fortunate enough to get a copy of from some records that she had donated to the Fort Bliss Museum. According to the author of this email[151], he was assigned to the 76th MP BN (PROV) and was assigned to patrol the Cemetery along with a partner.

On the night in question, they went in the gate and cruised to the rear of the cemetery which contained the most recent graves. As he was driving through the winding road that ran through the cemetery, he thought he saw something moving to his right. He naturally figured that he was seeing a person, as people liked to go into the cemetery to "park", so the author of the email began to look for the person he had seen and spotted what appeared to be a man running through the cemetery perpendicular to his path of travel.

Someone running in the cemetery was odd but not too odd as a lot of military personnel jog in the cool of the evening, however, in this particular instance, he could see headstones through the transparent body of the running figure. The running figure continued on a straight course through the cemetery and suddenly disappeared.

The email author was surprised at the figure that just vanished, but he was not really concerned until his partner asked if he had seen a running figure. Since they had both seen this person vanish, they stopped and car and began a thorough search of the area where the figure had last been seen, but they could not find any sign that anyone else was in the cemetery but themselves.

It had been raining earlier in the day and so it was somewhat overcast, with no moon or stars shining and it was around 2 or 3 in the morning. Even though the ground was somewhat muddy and should have retained footprints, there was no sign that anyone had run through the area.

---

[151] Heidi did not use his name in her writings so I will respect his privacy as well.

CHAPTER NINETEEN
VETERANS ADMINISTRATION
HEALTHCARE CENTER

The El Paso Veterans Administration Health Care Center is located at 5001 N. Piedras Street, in El Paso and is actually collocated with William Beaumont Army Medical Center.

Bernie Bellflower is the manager of the VA Canteen located on the second floor of the building. He told me about the incident when he arrived to open the cafeteria and found all of the trays that had been sitting on racks in the kitchen the night before laid on the floor in a very unusual pattern.

The Veterans Administration Medical Facility has motion sensors all throughout the various floor to detect intruders. Even though the mere motion of the trays moving should have set off the motion sensors, there was no sign that there had been any movement within or around the Canteen or the cafeteria.

Do spirits walk the hallways?

.

CHAPTER TWENTY
MCGREGOR RANGE

In an isolated empty building on McGregor Range, it is said that snatches of bawdy songs can still be heard from a time when this building was a smoke filled tavern, alive with the sounds of human camaraderie and the throaty sounds of female singers.

The stories that I have heard about McGregor Range have been many and fascinating, unfortunately, it is almost impossible to get any concrete information about the locations. It is as if they exist in some kind of vacuum. So this sent me on another search for information that had little in the way of success.

I had long heard about an old building on McGregor Range that that once was a stagecoach stop and then a theatre and watering hole called the Tumbleweed Tavern. It was a location once favored by soldiers and civilians alike who wanted to end a hard day's work by listening to painted women singing bawdy songs. It is now said that this old building is still frequented by the spirits of those who once enjoyed times of peace within its walls[152]. There are many stories of individuals hearing the old bawdy songs coming from the area that contains the old stage where the performances took place.

I am a little puzzled at some of the stories that I have heard about this location. I am told that what was the Tumbleweed Tavern is now designed as

---

[152] Coleman, Elaine, Texas Haunted Forts, Republic of Texas Press, Plano, Texas. 2001

Building 9464[153], the Asa P. Gray, Jr. Recreation Center, McGregor Range. If Building 9464 and the Tumbleweed Tavern are one and the same, building 9464 was not built until 1968[154], and it is of cinder block construction, so I find it difficult to reconcile this late building date with this structure having once been a stage stop, though there could have been an earlier building at this same location. The building does contain a stage where performances once took place, so perhaps the basic stories are true.

Today, what was the recreational center has been divided into sections that are used for various functions. At one end of the building there is the well known Tumbleweed Tavern that is still in use. At the other end there is a small post exchange for use by those stationed at McGregor Range. Another area in the building is used for administrative purposes and a small common area containing an automatic teller machine.

It appears, based on the fact that the name the Tumbleweed Tavern is still in use that the building's original purpose may have been as a recreation center. The building bore the name the Asa P. Gray, Jr. Recreation Center and some believe that the building was named in honor of the Gray Family that was very prominent in the early history of the land that became known as McGregor Range. However, the Asa P. Gray, Jr. after whom the building was named was not one of the old Gray family long associated with the land that became McGregor Range, but rather he was a Colonel in the United States Army who was killed in Vietnam in 1968.

Colonel Asa P. Gray, Jr. was born June 19, 1918 in Pennasen, Virginia and entered the Army from Michigan in 1940 with a commission in the Coastal Artillery. Colonel Gray served with Air Defense Artillery united during World War II and Korea. He graduated from the University of Maryland in 1964 with a BS degree in Military Science.

In the mid-sixties, Colonel Gray was sent to the Republic of Vietnam as an advisor to the Vietnamese Armed Forces. He was serving in this capacity on May 13, 1969 when he was killed in action. His decorations included the Silver Star, Legion of Merit with Oak Leaf Cluster, Bronze Star, Air medal with V-Device and two Oak Leaf Clusters, Joint Service Commendation Medal; Army Commendation Medal with Oak Leaf Custer, Vietnamese Cross of Gallantry with Palm Device and the Vietnamese National Order of Merit, Fifth Class.

Perhaps Colonel Gray himself returns to listen to the old songs with the spirits of the other honored dead who continue to make Fort Bliss their home. It would be a fitting tribute, I think.

---

[153] Patricia M. Rhodes, Air Defense Artillery Historian, Fort Bliss, Texas
[154] Daniel De LaHoy, Historical Architect, Fort Bliss, Texas

CHAPTER TWENTY-ONE
RED CANYON RANGE CAMP

This story doesn't really deal with a ghost, per se, but rather with a missing building. It is a true mystery of the desert that has never been solved. Now we all know that the United States Army has a paper trail on everything and everyone who has ever been associated with the Service, so I am sure that you will say that the Army does not lose buildings, however, I am here to tell you that in this particular case, records do show that the Army completely lost a Chapel. The entire building vanished like a wraith in the night, leaving only its foundations for all to see. The United States Army responsible for guarding the safety of the free world completely lost an entire building. Is nothing sacred?

Figure 47: Chapel at Red Canyon Range Camp[155]

Red Canyon was the forerunner of today's McGregor Guided Missile Range and it was started as a temporary firing area, to be used only until another location closer to Fort Bliss could be obtained. Red Canyon Range is actually in New Mexico and is closer to the city of Carrizozo, New Mexico than Fort Bliss, Texas. Red Canyon was the primary training area for soldiers training on and firing the Nike Ajax Missile. For over six years, the 400 men assigned to Red Canyon Range hosted over 800 battery-firings of the Nike and accommodated over 13,000 visitors to the site, including representatives from 45 foreign countries and 40 states[156].

---

[155] This picture is from the El Paso Times, July 23, 1964.
[156] El Paso Times, *Missing Range Camp Chapel Puzzles Army*, El Paso Times, July 23, 1964.

Figure 48: These steps are all that is left of the missing Chapel.

From the establishment of the Camp, troops had to attend church services in the post theater, since as a temporary camp Red Canyon Range was not authorized to have a chapel. However, never tell an American serviceman that he cannot have something that he has his heart set on obtaining.

In late 1957, Lieutenant Colonel John McCarthy, then commanding officer of Red Canyon Range and Master Sergeant William Sidell, Non-Commissioned Officer in Charge of the Range devised a plan for a chapel and turned the project over to the troops who accepted the challenge with great enthusiasm. The 103 men assigned to the range at that time, from 32 states including Hawaii and the Philippines, worked on the chapel from the laying of the first stone on December 16, 1957 until the completion of the Red Canyon Range Chapel on April 6, 1958. The soldiers spent off duty hours, weekends and holidays in gathering materials and building the building they so wanted[157].

The men were not able to use any Army funds in the construction of this unauthorized chapel, but they made use of such diverse materials as old railroad track, the old jail doors from Lincoln County, scrap metal and wood salvaged from crates use to ship solid propellant boosters for the Nike Ajax Missiles. Rock for the outside walls was quarried from the nearby hillsides. The front pillars were made from telephone poles covered with mortar while the windows were

---

[157] Ibid

given a stained glass effect by covering them with cellophane paper and several coats of shellac. Even the three bells that were used to call the men to services were missile booster cones heated by actual firing. It was said that this heating gave them a resonant tone[158]. Of all of the materials used in the church, only the shingles and the design affixed over the windows in the foyer were purchased using money contributed by the men of Red Canyon Range.

The effort by these men and the chapel that they were making out of "junk" as a place of worship so impressed the Chief of Army Chaplains, Major General Patrick J. Ryan, that he flew from Washington D.C. to personally dedicate the partially completed chapel on January 22, 1958[159]. During the dedication service, General Ryan stated that"

"This has the heart and soul of you men in it. This chapel is a monument to faith, and to every young man who comes into the chapel, God whispers, 'Without me you can do nothing. With me you can do all things'."

On Easter, April 6, 1958, the first service was held in the new chapel at Red Canyon Range. From that time until late 1959, the troops worshiped in the chapel that they had built with their own two hands as a symbol of their faith. Then all personnel were transferred to McGregor Range, leaving on a skeleton crew to run the camp and help salvage material[160].

All of the temporary buildings were removed from Red Canyon Range and the Quonset huts were transferred to other areas. When Master Sergeant Sidell, the last man to leave the canyon, walked out in the spring of 1961, only the Chapel, built by the sweat of the men as a place for them to worship their God, was left standing.

Somehow, someway, since that day in 1961, the Chapel at Red Canyon Range has completely vanished. According to the U.S. Army District Engineers office in Albuquerque, New Mexico, the agency in charge of the property at Red Canyon Range, the building was put up for sale, but the file on Red Canyon Range has been destroyed under Army Regulations.

A thorough search was conducted at the Real Estate Division at Fort Bliss, White Sands Missile Range, New Mexico and each of the men who had been stationed at Red Canyon Range was questioned. Unfortunately, no one knew anything about the fate of the Chapel built by the men of Red Canyon Range.

---

[158] Ibid
[159] Ibid
[160] Ibid

CHAPTER TWENTY-TWO
DONA ANA RANGE, NEW MEXICO

There are many mysteries to be found in the wide open prairie surrounding El Paso and Fort Bliss. One of these mysteries was revealed in December 1964 as a detail of soldiers from Fort Bliss searched New Mexico's Dona Ana Range, northeast of El Paso, for a downed artillery target drone[161]. They didn't find the artillery drone for which they searched, but they did unearth a small mystery when they stumbled across a weather worn grave marker. Finding a solitary marker standing alone on the lonely prairie brought everyone to a halt.

Slowly, one of the soldiers rubbed his hand across the worn lettering to clear it enough to be read. A close examination revealed the following inscription:

IN MEMORY OF PUP
21 YEARS OLD
DIED NOVEMBER 20, 1933
A WONDERFUL FRIEND
AND
COMPANION TO HIS MASTER
SGT. P.A. DANA

No one had any idea how the marker got to its location, when it was placed there or anything else about it. However, someone had heard of Sgt. P.A. Dana, so from that one fact, the rest of the story was found that was so carefully retold in the El Paso Times.

This story had its beginning in the year 1912 when the Army acquired a piece of land in New Mexico, near El Paso, but 32 miles from Fort Bliss. Since the property was situated in Dona Ana County, New Mexico, the Army called the Range the Dona Ana Target Range.

---

[161] El Paso Times, *Weather-Worn Grave Marker Brings to Light Dog's Life Story*, December 13, 1964.

Figure 49: Mysterious Grave Marker found on Dona Ana Range

The story of Pup actually begins in 1916 when Troop B of the 8th U.S. Cavalry, stationed in Marfa, Texas, obtained a Troop Mascot that they named Pup. When Troop B obtained their Mascot, Pup was a small dog of uncertain age, white in color. However, if the marker put up to his friend by Sgt. Dana was accurate, Pup was 14 years old when he became the Mascot of Troop B.

In October, 1919, the 8th Cavalry was transferred to Fort Bliss from Marfa and Pup successfully made the 225 overland march with his Troop. The First Sergeant of Troop B at that time was Paul A. Dana and he and Pup took a strong liking to each other during this long tiring trip. They settled into a peaceful routine in their new billets at fort Bliss.

Peace, unfortunately, was not to last as the Mexican Bandits began to raid into the United States. In response to these incursions, Troop B was detached and sent to serve at Fort Hancock. The Troop was assigned to patrol the Rio Grande from the fort, southeast to the Evetts Ranch and almost to Sierra Blanca. Pup continued to serve Troop B loyally, taking each step that his mounted friends took.

In 1922, Troop B returned to Fort Bliss and was informed that Dona Ana Range, which had been used on periodically, was now going to be opened and used year round. Sgt. Dana was offered the job of caretaker for the range and he accepted. His decision was certainly understandable as Sgt. Dana was offered a number of incentives, including his regular military pay plus a subsistence allowance of $1.00 a day and a ration allowance of .21 per day. In 1922, this was considered a substantial amount of money.

This tour of duty by Sgt. Dana as caretaker of Dona Ana Range marked what seemed to be a turning point in the life of this career soldier. Sergeant Dana had a somewhat unique career. He had enlisted in the cavalry in 1900 after completing two years of college. With the beginning of World War I, Sergeant Dana was commissioned as a Second Lieutenant and based on demonstrated ability he rose to the rank of Captain while serving in the Philippines. He was building a good solid career as an effective officer, but lurking around the corner was the "gratitude" of a grateful nation.

World War I was coming to a close and the nation wanted to forget about death and war and there was a move afoot to reduce the size of the standing army since World War I had been the war to end all wars. Therefore, as a first step, all officers who had been commissioned from the ranks were discharged. Sergeant Dana chose to reenlist in the 8th Cavalry and was assigned to Troop B, stationed in Marfa, Texas. In 1919, he became First Sergeant of the Troop.

Sergeant Dana was well liked by his subordinates and respected by most of his superiors as a meticulous soldier. His military bearing was above reproach, but there were some who said that he had a liking for the bottle. However, all being said, everyone agreed that Sergeant Dana was a good soldier.

When Sergeant Dana left for Dona Ana Range, he took his good friend, Pup, with him. He was also accompanied by a detail of three escort wagons, a mountain wagon, four mules and two riding horses. The soldiers assigned to the detail helped Dana set up his camp and then they left him on his own and returned to Fort Bliss.

Sergeant Dana did not lack for company while at Dona Ana Range. He had a number of other pets besides Pup during this time period, including cats, snakes and a coyote, but at no time did any visitor doubt that Pup was his favorite.

Figure 50: Troop B, 8th Cavalry on patrol accompanied by Pup, the mascot.

While Sergeant Dana was the caretaker at Dona Ana Range, he spent nine months of the year alone at the range, only coming back to Fort Bliss once a month to collect his pay and to replenish his supplies. The other three months of the year, the 1st Cavalry Division utilized the range for small arms training and the 82nd Field Artillery used the open range for firing their 75 millimeter guns. However, each unit only remained on the range for 3 or 4 weeks at a time.

According to the news article, Sergeant Peter J. Waraska of the 8th Cavalry's Troop A was on a hunting trip to Dona Ana Range on the day that Pup passed away, finally leaving the side of the man he had followed for over seven years. Sergeant Waraska said that Sergeant Dana was heartbroken at the death of his long time friend. Pup was given a full military funeral with all of the pomp and ceremony possible at the deserted range.

The death of his companion seemed to be a major turning point in the life of Sergeant Dana. Seven months after the death of Pup, he returned to Fort Bliss to retire as a master sergeant having spent 25 years of military service. However, due to his time spent in the Philippines, Sergeant Dana was credited with double time so that he actually retired with credit for 30 years of service.

From a Master Sergeant in the military, Sergeant Dana became a minister. He moved to the Pacific Northwest to minister to those living in that somewhat isolated region.

CHAPTER TWENTY-THREE
LOST TREASURES ASSOCIATED WITH FORT BLISS

THE TREASURE OF VICTORIO PEAK

The entire Fort Bliss complex is a sprawling installation and several adjunct facilities covering tens of thousands of acres of land in two states. One of these adjunct installations is White Sands Missile Range in New Mexico. According to many stories going back into the early part of the twentieth century a fantastic cache of treasure is hidden in the mountains that are located on this government facility.

According to information from the White Sands Public Affairs Office[162] in 1979 Ova Noss stood on the side of Victorio Peak posing for photos. During this photo session she told the group with her that, "Like they say, 'there's gold in them thar hills'." Ova Noss died later in 1979 but The Ova Noss Family Partnership is back on White Sands Missile Range seeking access to the legendary treasure.

One of the people accompanying Ova Noss in 1979 was Terry Delonas, her grandson. Delonas is the head of the family partnership and has been leading the effort to gain entry into Victorio Peak.

In early 1989 the partnership approached the Dept. of Army seeking permission to talk to White Sands about possible entry into Victorio Peak. Taking on much of the effort has been Norman Scott's Expeditions Unlimited out of Florida. Scott has been in the treasure hunting business for years and organized the hunt which took place at Victorio Peak in 1977.

For those of you unfamiliar with this story Victorio Peak is a small hill, about 400 feet high, in the Hembrillo Basin in the San Andres Mountains. The

---

[162] http://www.wsmr.army.mil/paopage/PAO.htm

peak is about five miles east of the missile range's western boundary and is almost directly west of the White Sands Space Harbor.

A man named Milton Noss, in 1937, supposedly found a treasure trove of Spanish gold and artifacts in a tunnel within the peak. He then claimed he accidentally sealed the tunnel in 1939 while trying to enlarge it---and another fabulous treasure was lost. But more about the history of this legend in next week's paper. It gets pretty good as it involves skeletons, jewels and gold bars the seekers say are now worth three billion dollars.

The Dept. of Army granted Terry Delonas and Norman Scott permission to talk to Maj. Gen. Thomas Jones, missile range commander. After listening to the presentation, the general told the group he would allow the exploration of Victorio Peak on two conditions. The first was that all the work be done on a noninterference basis. The second was that White Sands be directly reimbursed for any support it would provide.

The first condition was readily agreed to. While Victorio Peak sits in the mountains very near the range's boundary it is part of the Yonder Area, an Air Force gunnery range. When Air Force training missions as well as some missile firings are scheduled the searchers will have to evacuate the area.

The second condition was a little trickier. Suffice it to say the system did not allow the partnership to pay White Sands directly. The check would be made out to the U.S. Treasury and the money would disappear back East. The partnership approached Congressman Joe Skeen and he attached a rider to the Defense Authorization Act for 1990 which would allow direct reimbursement to the Army and WSMR[163].

With the signing of the money bill, Norman Scott, acting as Project Director for the partnership, arranged to conduct an environmental and engineering survey of Victorio Peak. He arrived on Jan. 8 to present the missile range with a check for $54,000 and to start the survey. The check was actually presented by Aaron Kin, a financial backer.

The money is to cover costs incurred by the range during the survey period. Some of this support includes security at the peak by the military police, scheduling by National Range, blading the old road by the Directorate for Engineering, Housing and Logistics and Public Affairs support for a press day at the peak.

During the two-week survey period the group was trying to figure out the best place to dig and, also, to conduct the required environmental work. To determine where the supposed treasure room might be Lambert Dolphin was back taking ground radar readings of the peak. Dolphin had a similar function during the gold search of 1977 and is under contract to Expeditions Unlimited. They also made infrared images of the peak and brought in a number of witnesses to try to determine where to dig.

---

[163] White Sands Missile Range

Les Smith, another man with a great deal of experience with Victorio Peak was also present to help. Smith accompanied Ova Noss to the peak in 1979 and was with the Gaddis Mining Company when it searched for the gold for 60 days in 1963.

The environmental work was contracted out by the partnership and is a key point yet. Contrary to what the press has said, the family partnership does not have final permission to dig at the peak. A license has been negotiated with the partnership but it has not been signed. It will not be signed until the required environmental documentation is satisfactorily completed.

Once the environmental work is completed and the license signed, the partnership will be allowed to work at the peak as long as they keep enough money in a White Sands fund to pay for range support. Jones has made it very clear he does not want the taxpayer to foot the bill for this search. The group claims it will have the environmental work complete in April.

During the two-week study period, Scott and Delonas brought in a number of potential contractors to bid on work which will have to be done at the peak.

On the 18th the missile range cooperated with the family partnership to give the press an opportunity to see and photograph Victorio Peak. The press representatives were mostly local except for the Denver Post and the Houston Chronicle.

The day started with a press conference at the Hilton Hotel in Las Cruces where Delonas and Scott introduced their key employees and supporters. In questioning by the press Delonas said the project will probably cost the partnership and its supporters from one to two million dollars.

At the peak, Ova Noss' two daughters, Letha Guthrie and Dorothy Delonas, and two grandsons, Terry and Jim Delonas, were continuously interviewed by members of the press. Letha and Dorothy told them about handling gold bars and Letha also told them how their stepfather once partially filled a glass jar with uncut rubies from the peak. No one asked where the rubies might have come from since there are no major deposits of rubies in North or South America.

SOME HISTORY OF VICTORIO PEAK

Stories of lost and buried treasure abound in the West. In New Mexico alone there are dozens of legends and stories dealing with gold and silver hidden away in the recesses of one mountain chain or another.

One of the newer and most popular stories (it comes close to rivaling the Lost Dutchman in the Superstition Mountains of Arizona) deals with Victorio Peak, right here on White Sands Missile Range. It is typical of all lost treasure stories in that there is little or no hard evidence, there are a few facts mixed in with an avalanche of rumor and for some reason the location is lost or it is somehow now inaccessible.

The Victorio Peak story begins in November 1937 when Milton E. Noss went hunting in the Hembrillo Basin of the San Andres Mountains. By the way, Noss is also called "Doc" because he often passed himself off as a doctor. He was not and was reportedly arrested in Texas for practicing medicine without a license.

While hunting Noss supposedly climbed Victorio Peak to take a look around. On his way up it began to rain and he took shelter in a natural opening on top. In a small room there he moved a large boulder and discovered a shaft leading down into the mountain.

He came back later with his wife Ova and climbed down into the shaft. He supposedly followed the faults in the peak down several hundred feet until he found a large room. After exploring the large room and several other small ones he returned to the surface.

By most of the accounts, he reported to Ova he had found a room large enough to drive a train into. Through it, a stream of cold water ran. There were chests filled with Spanish coins, jewelry and religious artifacts. Also, there were Spanish documents, Wells Fargo chests and thousands of gold bars stacked like wood. Finally, there were 27 skeletons tethered to the floor.

Understandably, the value of this treasure has grown over the years with inflation and the increased value of gold. Years ago some estimated its value at 26 million dollars. Now the Noss family says it may be worth three billion dollars. Funny thing about inflation though. All those original reports say there were 27 skeletons. Now, in one report, the family is saying there are 79 bony guardians down there.

From 1937 to 1939 Noss and his wife supposedly worked to bring the treasure to the surface. During this time Noss worked diligently hauling up bars and hiding them all around the region. He never let Ova go down into the treasure chamber and he always hid the bars himself. Some say he didn't trust anyone. She claimed he was worried about her getting hurt or kidnapped.

Apparently there was some sort of choke point in the fissure which made it difficult getting out with the loot. So Noss hired a mining engineer to dynamite that point and enlarge it. Too much explosive was used and the "squeeze" was blasted shut. Efforts to open the shaft or bypass it proved futile.

Before we continue this story we have to consider where this alleged treasure may have come from. The most written about and talked about source has to be the legendary Padre La Rue mine.

This legend is usually associated with the Organ Mountains, but Victorio Peak is only 40 miles to the north. Around 1800 there was a young priest named La Rue who ministered to a small Indian tribe in Mexico. He befriended an old Spanish soldier who, on his deathbed, told La Rue about a fabulous vein of gold just two days north of Paso Del Norte (El Paso).

Because the crops were failing and the Indians starving, the padre led the group to this area and found the rich vein. What they found to eat I don't know, but the story says they did mine the gold for several years.

The Spanish sent soldiers to find out what had happened to the padre. When La Rue heard they were near he had the Indians hide the gold and all evidence of the mine. They were then captured by the Spanish who killed the padre and all his followers in a vain attempt to find the location to the mine.

Many people will have you believe that Noss found the original mine, while others say it is just the secret hiding place. Ova did produce a photograph of some gold bars which Doc brought up and one is clearly stamped with the name "La Rue." Could Victorio be the site of the original mine or the hiding place with the mine located somewhere in the vicinity? I like numbers---let me throw some at you.

Expeditions Unlimited had an assay done of the sandstone in Victorio Peak and it came back showing one tenth of an ounce of gold in each ton of rock. To get 100 tons of gold (a number usually cited by supporters based on the number of bars reported) from a site with this concentration of gold would require crushing and processing 32 million tons of rock. In South Dakota, the Homestake Mine is the most profitable and longest lived gold mine in the Western Hemisphere. There the gold assay is two and a half times richer than the sample from Victorio Peak and it has taken them a century to extract 1,000 tons of gold---using modern explosives and equipment, I might add.

A ton of ore in the South Dakota mine is equal to about 19 cubic feet. If rocks are similar in the Victorio Peak area we are talking about removing and processing over six hundred million cubic feet of rock or a pile of rock the size of a football field and over two miles high. Where do you suppose the padre hid it?

OK, OK, maybe ore that poor isn't a fair test. Let's say the ore the padre mined was 100 times richer. No, let's say it was 1,000 times richer or had an assay of 100 ounces of gold per ton of rock. Doing the same calculations we end up with a pile of mine tailings the size of a football field and 12.5 feet high. If it was in the San Andres Mountains, I bet we could find it.

Another story which avoids these unpleasant numbers deals with Emperor Maximilian of Mexico. According to this story, he was trying to flee Mexico with all of his riches. The mules made it and the stash was hidden with the porters being left to die in the cave. Unfortunately for Maximilian, he didn't make it out of Mexico.

A third story has the German government sending a shipment of gold over to Pancho Villa and the gold being waylaid in New Mexico. The gold was supposed to be used by Villa to pay for his attacks against the United States and draw the U.S. into war with Mexico so the Americans would not go to Europe and fight in World War I.

The fourth explanation for gold in Victorio Peak is the one about it being a repository for Apache raiders. This would explain the Wells Fargo chests found down there by Noss.

Then there are the combo explanations which marry a couple of these into one story. One of the most persistent is that La Rue's gold is down there and the Apaches also used it to store their loot. This explains the Mescalero Apache interest in the gold hunts at Victorio Peak. They claim any gold found in the peak rightly belongs to them since they stole it and then hid it in the peak during the 19th Century for safekeeping.

Once Noss blew up the entrance to the treasure room the story of the peak gets more complicated with a variety of helpers, witnesses and financial backers. Noss is reported to have already removed hundreds of gold bars from the mountain as well as a great deal of jewelry and other artifacts. Sure, it was illegal to own gold in those days but no one has really explained why Noss needed financial backers to dig out the debris in the tunnel. The jewelry, including those uncut rubies Letha mentioned, surely could have been turned into lots of instant cash.

Anyway, Noss had a number allies working at the peak. In 1941 a group of about 20 people, who had furnished money and labor, formed a company to raise money to straighten up and timber the shaft.

During the war Noss disappeared and divorced Ova while he was living in Arkansas. He came back in 1945 and the small group wanted to incorporate but Noss refused.

Noss turned up again in 1949 working for Charley Ryan in Alice, Texas. Noss supposedly talked Ryan into traveling with him to New Mexico to check on "the mine." When they got to Victorio Peak they found Ova controlling the site with a state permit which allowed her to prospect there. Noss allegedly told Ryan not to worry and they filed claims on sites north of Victorio Peak which contain some lead bearing ore.

According to court testimony, Ryan finally realized he was being duped by Noss into providing money for nothing. Ryan testified he stopped his lead mining operations on March 4 and 5, 1949 and told Noss he was leaving New Mexico after he called the sheriff to come and arrest Noss for fraud.

Noss struck Ryan and ran out of the Ryan house in Hatch and shouted he would kill them all. Ryan stepped out on the porch and fired two shots from his own pistol. The second shot hit Noss in the head and killed him instantly.

Ryan's murder trial was held on May 25 and 26 in Las Cruces. The jury brought in a verdict of not guilty based on self defense.

There wasn't much testimony about buried treasure during the trial. Ova supposedly claimed there was a conspiracy of silence and Doc was killed over gold bars he didn't deliver. One source says Ryan later went to Ova and proposed a partnership in Victorio Peak. She refused.

The press reports all say Ryan killed Noss because he wouldn't turn over gold he promised to sell to Ryan. The trial testimony doesn't raise this issue. I suppose there could have been a cover up but it seems just as plausible that Ryan told the truth during the trial. There is probably a little bit of truth in both sides.

We do know Ryan later received lease payments from White Sands for the lead mining claims. He had 13 claims when the missile range took over the land around Victorio Peak and he was paid $300 per year.

Next---more Victorio Peak stories with Capt. Fiege and the Air Force connection and hard rock mining with the Gaddis Mining Company.

After Doc's death Ova Noss inherited the story of treasure at Victorio Peak and its inherent benefits and curses. She continued to work at the peak with the help of supporters and family members and to sell shares.

In 1952 she visited the Denver Mint and inquired if Milton Noss had made any deposits of gold at the Mint from November 1937 to March 1949. Mint records showed none was made. Interestingly she wrote the Mint in 1939 asking officials what they should do if they found gold. She indicated they had an old map showing the location of gold bars and they were searching for them. She was told to notify the Mint immediately if they found anything.

Another interesting fact from 1939 involving the Mint is a "gold brick" which was submitted to the U.S. Treasury for assay by Charles Ussher of Santa Monica, Calif. He supposedly paid $200 for the brick which he obtained from a man named Grogan. The assay revealed the bar contained 97 cents of gold. In an investigation conducted by the Secret Service, Grogan revealed he obtained the "gold brick" from Doc Noss in New Mexico.

On July 13, 1950 the Army entered a lease agreement with Roy Henderson for the land where Victorio Peak is located. Many people don't realize there was a goat ranch right at the foot of Victorio Peak. The Henderson family lived there and before that it was grazed periodically by the Gilmore family. In fact, in 1973, Mart Gilmore said he took Noss to Hembrillo Basin in 1936 to show him a cave---at the request of Noss.

This was originally state land and the U.S. Government was granted the use of the land "for any military purpose whatsoever."

A search of records by officials in December 1950 revealed there were no existing legal mining claims in the area. On November 14, 1951 Public Land Order No. 703 was issued which withdrew all WSMR lands from prospecting, entry, location and purchase under mining laws and reserved their use for military purposes.

Interestingly, on January 5, 1953 Ova Noss assigned four percent of her Victorio Peak interests to J. L. Fowler of Enid, Oklahoma, who, in turn, sold parts to at least 10 persons in Oklahoma and Kansas. In February 1955, a Mrs. Miller of Caldwell, Texas wrote to the Mint concerning the purchase of gold mining stock from Ova Noss. This is intriguing since public records showed Ova had no legal claims at the peak. There is some correspondence showing the Treasury Department was concerned about the possibility of fraud and an investigation was made.

The next highlight in the story of Victorio Peak is the Fiege episode. Leonard Fiege was an Air Force captain assigned to Holloman AFB in 1958. He later claimed in 1961 that he and three men--Berclett, Prather and Wessel--went hunting in the Hembrillo Basin in 1958 and stumbled upon a tunnel in Victorio Peak. Fiege and Berclett claimed they crawled through it into a small room which contained a stack of gold bars. Berclett recently admitted in a press interview they were hunting gold to begin with, not wildlife.

Not to jeopardize their positions with the military, these two bright guys claimed they did not remove any of the gold. NOTE: Lost treasure stories always have a lot in common with horror movies. The participants never seem to be too bright and they never learn from past stories which clearly tell us not to open the closet door when creepy things are happening and to take some of the gold with you when you find it.

Berclett still claims he scratched his initials on one of the bars. They then spent several hours caving in the entrance to the little room so no one would find it.

In May 1961 the WSMR commander received a letter from the Holloman commanding general requesting Fiege and partners under a Col. Garman's supervision be allowed to enter Victorio Peak to "get evidence which they will then provide to U.S. Treasury activities." On May 29 Fiege and group met with Maj. Gen. Shinkle, the WSMR CG, and Fiege stated it would be a simple matter to recover a few bars of gold. The request was denied.

At the end of June a group which included Fiege, Berclett and Colonels Garman and Gasiewicz from Holloman visited the director of the Mint and pleaded their case. As a result of that meeting the director sent a letter to the Secretary of the Army stating the Mint had been bothered a great deal by the gold story at Victorio Peak. He told the secretary they might be able to put an end to the rumors if the group was allowed to dig in the supposed tunnel.

The Secret Service had indicated earlier that there might be a cache of non-gold bars on the site which they said may have been placed there by Doc Noss to further his bunco game.

An old timer from El Paso calls me periodically to talk about Victorio Peak. He claims he knew Noss and that Noss used to buy copper bars in Oro Grande and have them electroplated with gold in El Paso. When asked why he doesn't tell his story to the press, he says he doesn't think they would care. It would spoil the story.

Another old timer who ranched near Victorio Peak claims Noss used to salt the sand at the springs around the base of the peak. When prospective investors showed up, Doc would be panning flakes of gold out of the sand at the spring.

When the Department of Army received the letter from the Mint, officials asked for the WSMR CG's comments. He said, "My stand has been that I shall deny entry...unless I obtain such permission. I desire this permission...and would like these rumors laid to rest." On July 30, 1961 Shinkle received permission to allow the investigation.

As we go through this scenario, you might want to keep in mind that this is the same operation which television's "Unsolved Mysteries" claimed only four people knew about.

So, on August 5 a group including Shinkle, Garman, Fiege, Berclett, Prather, Wessel, Major Robert Kelly, a number of WSMR military police and Special Agent L. E. Boggs of the Treasury Department went to Victorio Peak. For five days Fiege and his three partners worked to enter the tunnel but failed. At that point Shinkle told them to go away.

The Fiege group came back to Shinkle in August and September stating they would like to continue and was willing to work on weekends only. On September 20 Shinkle notified the Secret Service he was going to give Fiege more time but they would be restricted to the same tunnel. No new excavations would be allowed.

Work then continued on an intermittent basis for about five weeks under the surveillance of Capt. Swanner. In late October WSMR records indicate two men named Bradley and Gray entered Hembrillo Basin and approached the workers. Swanner supposedly ordered them to leave the missile range since they were trespassing. They demanded a piece of the action or they said they would tell Mrs. Noss. Swanner told them to leave.

On November 1 the state land commissioner notified the Army that Mrs. Noss was accusing them of mining her treasure. Things came quickly to a head and Shinkle ordered all work to stop on November 3.

Shinkle communicated with the Secretary of the Army and local officials that work was stopped and that the Fiege group had found nothing. The Secret Service already knew it since they had a man on site. The Noss lawyers pushed for access for Mrs. Noss. On December 6, with advice from a long list of other agencies, Shinkle excluded all persons from the range not directly engaged in conducting missile tests.

By the way, the fact that Capt. Swanner's name is on the walls of one of the fissures in Victorio Peak is not the big deal that "Unsolved Mysteries" made it to be on Sunday night. According to Don Swann of Las Cruces, who was stationed at WSMR in 1956, soldiers were always spending weekends and free time in places like Victorio Peak. He says he put his name in one of the peak's tunnels as did the soldiers with him. It is sometimes called "soldiers hole."

At this point we need to make a clarification or fine distinction involving the Army's activity during the Fiege episode. The press pounces on this and often says the Army admits it did work at the site. This is not the case. The Army allowed a claimant to do work at the site. The Army does not admit that it conducted any kind of official or unofficial search at the peak for its own benefit.

After this the Noss group continued to seek permission to enter. The range's position was that the group had no legal claim; therefore there was no reason to grant such an entry.

In late 1962 the Gaddis Mining Company and the New Mexico Museum approached the missile range seeking permission to enter and dig at Victorio Peak. The state of New Mexico sponsored the request and the Army recognized the state's interest in a possible historical find. Rumors flew during the dig saying

Harold Beckwith, son of Ova Noss, was financing Gaddis. On June 20, 1963 a license was granted by the Army for a 30-day exploration.

The work began with simultaneous archaeological, seismic and gravity surveys. According to Chester Johnson, a museum rep on site, nothing was found. He added that "a D7 caterpillar was used to cut and build roads where ever they were needed, even on top of the peak." Most of the scars on the peak are a result of this activity, not any Army work at the site.

The roads and platforms were necessary for placing a drilling rig. According to Johnson, the rig, "using a 4.5 inch rock bit and drilling with air, was used to test the anomalies (those places indicated by survey that might be caverns). Drill holes varied from 18 to 175 feet in depth, depending on location....There were about 80 holes drilled during the project."

In addition to this work the company drove their own tunnel 218 feet into the side of Victorio Peak in an attempt to gain access to the lower regions. This failed.

To accomplish all this, the State had to request an extension which was granted. The 30-day extension made the exploration period July 19 through September 17.

In the end the company found nothing and reportedly spent $250,000. As part of it White Sands filed a claim with the state for reimbursement for support during the quest. The claim for $7,640.54 was filed in October 1963 and finally paid in November 1964.

You might theorize after a mining company had spent two months on Victorio Peak without results, most people would realize gold bars don't grow out of the ground there. On the contrary, more dreamers rushed into the breach and came forward seeking quick riches from the uncooperative Army.

In 1964 and 1965 the Museum of New Mexico and Gaddis Mining were both back seeking permission to reenter the range. In the same period D. Richardson and R. Tyler visited White Sands requesting permission to locate "lost treasure."

Also, Violet Yancy, Doc Noss' second wife, showed up asking to get onto the range. Violet popped up again in 1969 making headlines in Texas and New Mexico. She hired two Fort Worth lawyers and was trying to establish her right to the treasure. She indicated there was documentation showing Doc left her 76 percent of the treasure and Ova the other 24 percent.

One person conspicuously missing from the recorded requests during the sixties is Ova Noss. More than likely she was operating through various backers at this time. A hot rumor during the Gaddis search was that Harold Beckwith, Ova's son, was financing the Gaddis operation. Reporters pressed the question at the time but could not confirm it. It may be the family was operating through some other group.

In 1968 E. F. Atkins and party started a series of requests and petitions which carried on for years. This was a persistent group which pulled out all the stops in trying to get in.

Senator Barry Goldwater wrote requesting permission for the Birdcage Museum of Arizona to explore for treasure. It was determined the museum and Atkins were one in the same. They supposedly also sought entrance through the cooperation of a man named Gill with ABC-TV.

Then the range received a letter from the Great Plains Historical Association of Lawton, Oklahoma which stated they had accepted scientific sponsorship of a treasure project at WSMR as outlined by an E. F. Atkins.

When all this was denied, Atkins asked for reconsideration and stated several Washington Army Authorities and senators and representatives had recommended approval. On checking with the Department of Army, WSMR learned the Secretary of Army had made no commitment and would back WSMR's decision 100 percent.

This cat and mouse game went on for years. In August 1971, The Department of Army indicated it had already received 55 Congressional inquiries that year on the behalf of Atkins and his request to search for gold. In a 1972 memo for record one range official noted he had received another request from Atkins to explore for gold. He indicated Atkins wanted to get together on a friendly basis and maybe something could be worked out so Atkins did not have to exert Congressional pressure on the Department of Army to gain access to WSMR. He did not get on White Sands.

This brings us to the point where Victorio Peak gained national exposure through the Watergate hearings and the likes of Jack Anderson and F. Lee Bailey.

On June 2, 1973, Jack Anderson reported in his syndicated column the story of noted attorney F. Lee Bailey's involvement with gold bars in New Mexico and specifically, White Sands Missile Range. According to Anderson, Bailey was authorized by a consortium to gain legal possession of the golden treasure at WSMR. The group promised to pay taxes and then sell the rest of the gold at a profit to themselves.

Bailey was supposedly skeptical at first so he asked for proof. The group came up with a gold bar about four inches long and promised hundreds more to prove their claim. Bailey sent it to the Treasury Department and had it assayed. It proved to be 60 percent gold and 40 percent copper. Anderson's article quickly pointed out ancient gold ingots often were not pure, and this percentage shouldn't be viewed as significant.

A Bailey spokesman later stated the consortium knew the location of 292 gold bars, each weighing about 80 pounds. However, Treasury and Army expressed disinterest in Bailey's proposals.

The bar given to Bailey was obviously not one of the alleged 80 pounders. An 80-pound bar with the stated proportion of gold and copper would be about 12 inches long, five inches wide and three inches thick. Interestingly, modern 14-karat gold jewelry is 58 percent gold and 42 percent other metals such as copper. In 1974 the same bar was examined by Los Alamos which came to the same conclusion. The press dutifully reported experts saying the bar was basically the same as jeweler's gold.

I suppose because he is well connected, Bailey took his problems to U.S. Attorney General John Mitchell. Mitchell then repeated much of it at a lunch with H.R. Haldeman and John Dean. Finally, Dean, during his Senate Watergate Investigation testimony, mentioned something about Bailey, gold bars in New Mexico and making a deal for his client to avoid prosecution for holding gold.

As with any story repeated several times, by the time Dean told it there was some distortion---according to Bailey's people. After a storm of Watergate headlines linking treasure to the investigation, Bailey's people said there were actually two groups of people. One was a small group which had stumbled onto the gold and the other was a group of businessmen supporting them.

Bailey never would reveal who his clients were but it later came out one was a Fred Drolte wanted by authorities on an arms smuggling charge. Bailey later was quoted as saying that given a helicopter and access to White Sands he could have gold bars in 30 minutes.

At this point things really started to get interesting. In late 1973 several people stole into the Hembrillo Basin and set off a dynamite charge in a side canyon east of Victorio Peak. They supposedly blasted the Indian pictographs off of a rock wall. Some people claimed if you knew how to read the drawings they would guide you to the treasure.

After the trespass, security was beefed up and a house trailer was put in at HELL site just west of Victorio Peak. It was to house range riders and military police. In July 1974 the range announced it was making more improvements to the site with the addition of a helicopter pad, a 30-foot antenna and portable generators. The additional work was done in anticipation of approval for another gold search.

At this point Victorio Peak was in the news all the time. There was lots of maneuvering by various groups trying to gain entrance. The Bailey group signed a deal with the state (New Mexico would get 25 percent) to allow them first crack at the peak. The Army didn't buy it and New Mexico battled the Army in the press for quite a while. At the time it must have been very serious for the two sides. But looking back on it and seeing how it was played out in the press, it looks pretty humorous---especially when you consider no one ever came up with anything approaching a whole gold bar and the basis for the whole argument anyway was the story of a man arrested for practicing medicine without a license.

As the story grew in the mid 70s a kind of gold fever or hysteria developed with it. The Bailey group starting claiming thousands of bars of gold, not just 292. Maybe it was the oil crisis, but somehow inflation kicked in and the treasure's worth grew to 225 billion dollars. The Washington Post came to the rescue and rationally pointed out Fort Knox only stored 6.2 billion dollars in gold reserves.

As the story spread the missile range started receiving letters from people all over the world asking for information or permission to explore. Perfect strangers came forward to offer their ESP capabilities, their divining rods, their great grandfather's knowledge and their old maps.

Some supposedly legitimate claimants emerged from this. In August 1973 White Sands received a letter from a lawyer named W. Doyle Elliott. It turns out he was retained by Roscoe Parr to get himself a piece of the action. Elliott stated in his letter that Parr, "alone possesses all of the necessary information and instructions from Dr. Noss to," settle the issue. The letter goes on to say Noss had an insight he might die before gaining access into the peak again and gave Parr all the necessary instructions to access the gold. Also he supposedly told Parr how to divide the treasure and generously offered Parr the balance after it was divided. Elliott solemnly pointed out Parr, "accepted and agreed to fulfill the requests made of him by Dr. Noss." None of this was apparently in writing.

By the end of 1974 you needed a program to keep all the claimants straight.

Someone reported Fiege had gone into partnership with Violet Noss Yancy. There also was the mysterious Bailey group, Ova Noss, Parr, the Shriver group, the "Goldfinder" group and Expeditions Unlimited headed by Norm Scott. Ova Noss took the bull by the horns and sued the Army for one billion dollars. The case was dismissed.

The Army was reluctant to deal with any one group for fear of showing favoritism. A number of solutions were proposed which included a lottery drawing to determine order of entry and a free-for-all gold rush which probably would have ended in a blood bath. None of these approaches was acceptable. Then Scott was able to organize the various claimants and he proposed Expeditions Unlimited represent the various groups and deal with exploring their claims.

The Army accepted and the search was set for mid 1976. This was postponed twice and, finally, "Operation Goldfinder" got underway in March 1977. It was put up or shut up time for most of the claimants.

Before it even started the range had to battle the rumors. Just a few days before the start word got around that the search was open to the public. Public Affairs scrambled to get the word out that only authorized searchers and press would be allowed in.

A press conference was held on March 18 and the actual search began the next day. Each day, press and searchers were registered at the peak and searched. At one point there was a report one of the claimant groups was going to try to salt the site. They were asked to leave by Scott. The searchers went site to site seeking the elusive gold bars. Eventually, an extension was granted to run the operation until April 1.

To say there was some press interest in the event would be an understatement. The New York Times, Washington Post, Los Angeles Times, London Daily Mail, Newsweek, Time Magazine, Rolling Stone and the National Enquirer were all there along with the local and regional print media. Of course, the television and radio stations showed up in force too. Probably the most notable, or, at least, most famous reporter attending was Dan Rather then with "60 Minutes." He attracted almost as much attention as the peak itself.

In the end most of the claimants had their time on Victorio and failed to turn up any gold bars---or anything of value. Immediately following the 1977 search there was a flurry of requests to reenter the range but the Department of Army emphatically stated, "That no exploration for lost treasure on WSMR will be permitted for the foreseeable future."

With the "foreseeable future" now behind us it is going to be interesting watching what happens during the next year at Victorio Peak. Recently, several people have said Doc Noss must be laughing in his grave. Henry James, in his book The Curse of the San Andres, said Victorio Peak was a haunting place with unusual sounds. Maybe he was only hearing a distant chuckle.

The 200-plus page environmental assessment for the search into Victorio Peak arrived at White Sands on June 14, 1990. The Plan was called, _An Environmental Assessment of The Ova Noss Family Partnership Expedition into Victorio Peak_, and was prepared by EcoPlan, Inc. of Albuquerque with the archaeological work being done by Human Systems Research, Inc. of Mesilla.

In the general description of the document it states, "There are several clearly defined steps to complete this operation." The steps are:

1) Improve the roads so drilling equipment can be put on the peak;
2) Locate and define the treasure cavern by drilling bore holes and using ground sensing radar;
3) Get to the cavern by tunneling or boring;
4) Explore the cavern for treasure and cultural antiquities;
5) Document and remove anything found;
6) Close all entrances to the peak;
7) Restore the landscape by approved reclamation methods.

To get the heavy equipment to the peak, the road will have to be improved. Currently, only high clearance vehicles with a relatively short wheel base can negotiate the hairpin curves and only four-wheel drive vehicles can actually get on the peak. The partnership proposed widening the road to a width of 15 feet.

Once on the peak, the group will use drilling equipment to put down a maximum of 10 bore holes which will be four to six inches in diameter. These holes will be drilled on the west and northwest slopes of the peak and will penetrate to a depth of up to 400 feet. These bore holes will allow the placement of the ground radar sensors deep in the peak and, if they penetrate the cavern, a small camera can be lowered to examine the cavity.

Once the partnership defines where the cavern is, they have proposed two possible methods of getting to it. One is to bore a hole straight through the limestone to the cave. This would involve erecting a 140-foot rig and drilling a

42-inch hole. The bits would be water cooled with trucked in tap water to avoid possible contamination of ground water.

They would run a pair of 600-horsepower air compressors which would remove cuttings from the hole. The document goes into some detail discussing the noise this machinery would make in the area. At its maximum, the noise would measure 85 to 87 decibels in the immediate area. They do not compare this to the noise made by Air Force jets which regularly maneuver in the Yonder Area gunnery range which is immediately over Victorio Peak.

This boring operation would run 24 hours a day with an estimated progress of eight to 16 feet per day. They estimate it will take 20 to 50 days to penetrate 400 feet into Victorio.

Once they reach the cavern a 36-inch steel sleeve would be inserted into the hole. This would allow access to the room. On completion of the operation, the partnership says it can weld a lid on the sleeve and cover it with dirt or backfill the sleeve itself and cover it.

The second and preferred method of gaining access to the cave is traditional tunneling. First, they plan to open seven existing holes to see if any can be used to shorten the distance to the cavern and reduce the amount of work needed.

The seven holes they plan to look at are: Porter-McDonald Tunnel, Soldiers Hole, Gaddis Tunnel, Upper Noss Shaft, Ova Noss Intercept, the West Lower Entry and Trench 1 Entry. These are all on the west and north sides of the peak. They do not mention using the Mule Hole or the Berlett-Fiege Hole.

The tunnel would be about 6x8 to 8x8 feet in diameter, as long as 400 feet in length and unsupported. They plan to use a Roadheader tunneling machine which grinds itself into the rock using circulating rotary heads which have a compressive strength of 10,000 psi. The machine uses a conveyor belt system to move the cuttings.

If the big machine doesn't work because of the hardness of the rock, it will be moved and the work continued using the drill and blast technique. This is classic hard rock tunneling. Holes are drilled into the facing wall. Explosives are inserted into the holes and detonated. The debris is then removed by hand or machine.

The document says by working two 12-hour shifts the workers should be able to advance eight to 16 feet per day.

Once the tunnel is completed, visitors would simply be able to walk to the cavern. After the operation is complete the partnership proposes backfilling the tunnel with the tailings.

In addition to the proposed "how to" information in the environmental assessment there is a great deal of data on the natural and cultural background of the area. For instance, the area is made mostly of Paleozoic sedimentary rock which is about 290 million years old. This includes shales, limestones, sandstones and reef material.

Apparently about 290 million years ago this area was under a large shallow marine sea known as the Virgillian Basin. It was a swampy, tropical lowland with shallow, brackish water. As the sea rose at one point a reef gradually grew in certain areas. A reef now caps Victorio Peak as the surrounding material has eroded away.

Because the sea was so shallow there are both marine and land plant fossils found on Victorio Peak.

The assessment lists hundreds of "potential species" to be found around Victorio Peak. This includes mammals such as mule deer and bobcat and everything down to octillo and sunflowers.

The document states, "No Federal Endangered or Threatened Species are expected at Victorio Peak. However, there was potential habitat for three State Endangered Plants and five State Sensitive plants as well as two State Endangered Animals."

The animals are the desert bighorn sheep and the gray vireo (a small songbird). None were documented at the peak. Of the state endangered and/or sensitive plants, four were actually found on the peak. They are Sandberg's pincushion, button cactus, rock daisy and the Threadleaf horsebrush.

Human Systems Research did the archaeology for the report and it provides interesting information on the area. It says human occupation of the San Andres Mountains extends from the PaleoIndian era (12,000 to 8,000 B.C.) to the present. It states, "Doubtless, many thousands of sites occur in the White Sands Missile Range."

The report talks about five sites at Victorio Peak. The three around the base include two prehistoric sites and the Henderson goat ranch found at the foot of the peak. The other two sites are on the peak and are a badly disturbed prehistoric site and the mining and treasure hunting work on the hill.

On the east side of the peak in a rock outcropping is a cross which is about four feet high and three feet wide. There are many legends dealing with this cross as many people feel it is a manmade marker for the treasure. The scientists say in the report that the horizontal bar is formed by the action of acidic water much like water dissolves limestone to form cave decorations. The vertical line of the cross is merely staining caused by water running down the rock in the same path for centuries.

Also near the cross is a crevice which is coated with a black material. Legend has it this is soot deposited by smoke from Padre La Rue's furnaces inside the mountain when he mined the gold there. More than likely it is simply oxidation of minerals found in the limestone and the assessment acknowledges this when the subject is discussed.

There is much more in the report. It defines in great detail the affected environment and then devotes almost 40 pages to expected impacts and what mitigative measures the partnership plans. There also is a section on reclamation.

Is it a good report? I can't answer that question. It has been sent to a long list of state and federal agencies which are required to comment on the assessment. In addition, the White Sands Environmental Office will evaluate it. Once that is done, we will have an idea of how complete the assessment is.

After all these experts have a crack at the report, it will be available to the public for comments.

According to Bob Burton, WSMR archaeologist, it will probably take until September to get all these reviews and commentary periods completed. He estimated they might have permission to dig by the end of September, if few changes are required.

The clock measuring the one year allowed for the treasure trove search at Victorio Peak will begin ticking on May 15.

That is one of the first things spelled out in the Army's licensing agreement which was signed April 4 by Terry Delonas and Brig. Gen. Ronald Hite. Delonas signed for the Ova Noss Family Partnership and Hite, as commanding general of WSMR, signed for the Department of Army.

In addition to the timeframe, the 16-page document limits the search area to a one mile radius of Victorio Peak, says the exploration will be without cost to the Government and the work will not interfere with other missile range activities. There also are paragraphs and subparagraphs outlining a variety of requirements ranging from a $200,000 deposit to lists of treasure locations and on-site participants.

The agreement goes to some length to make a distinction between what constitutes treasure versus artifacts. Paragraph 12 states, "All archeological resources, antiquities, or items of historical or cultural interest....whenever located on WSMR shall remain the property of the Government."

After this statement there is a long laundry list of what might be considered an artifact. It includes such common items as mortars, baskets, pottery, rock carvings, arrow heads and jewelry. The list was obviously lifted from a generic license because it includes, "all portions of shipwrecks." It seems unlikely a shipwreck will be found within Victorio Peak.

Now for the interesting part. The paragraph goes on to define "treasure" as "coins, gold or silver bullion, precious metals (not including metals with radioactive value), precious cut and uncut gems (not including jewelry or gems set in valuable ornaments), unset and loose jewels, and related valuables."

So, what happens if anything is found? The agreement says the partnership will cease operations immediately. Together, representatives of WSMR and the partnership will make a written and photographic inventory. The two parties will then categorize items as artifacts or treasure or neither with WSMR having the final determination in the matter.

Artifacts will then be dealt with by WSMR according to federal law. Treasure will be removed by the partnership under the direction of WSMR personnel.

At the signing Delonas said they were checking on vault storage with several banks in the area just in case something is discovered.

After removing the treasure, if any is found, the Department of Army will take custody of it. Following another inventory, the Army will, through the Department of Justice, go to the United States District Court for the District of New Mexico and request a determination as to the ownership of the treasure. Any subsequent court proceedings will certainly be fodder for the "entertainment-news" programs.

Another interesting requirement of the license is that "neither the Licensee nor any individual or company shall sell participation interests in the project contemplated by this license or in any manner utilize this license to prospect without first disclosing such transaction(s) to the Secretary of the Army." This portion of the license is intended to prevent anyone from implying that the Army endorses or backs the search.

To control the site and prevent any possible misrepresentation or fraud, all representatives of the partnership must consent "to a thorough search of their persons, vehicles, equipment, and any other personal property by Government security personnel." This includes a search prior to entry to the area or entry into any cavern or tunnel and a search on returning or emerging.

After the signing, Delonas said he could not say when the first activity would start. He did confirm that their first efforts will be directed at drilling small holes into the peak and then lowering cameras down the shafts.

He said they have developed a very sophisticated camera apparatus which contains video and still cameras and lights. They will be able to lower one device and control it from the surface to obtain live television video and 35-millimeter still photos.

He indicated this will probably take a few weeks and they will then withdraw to digest the data they collect. What they find will dictate how they will finally approach the peak for a full blown attempt to gain entry to any particular cavern.

In talking with Delonas after the signing he revealed he has a sense of humor---really a bit of black humor. He said he was happy the end of the search was finally in sight because all of his efforts during the past years had basically ruined his life.

Laughingly, he went on to say one of their financial backers was connected with the movie industry. This backer told Delonas the story would make a better movie if nothing was found. The movie could then portray a man who had wasted his life on nothing. It would be a tragedy and, after all, most of the greatest stories ever written were tragedies.

According to the Ova Noss Family Partnership, getting into the Victorio Peak cavern where Doc Noss supposedly found a king's ransom in gold and treasure may not be as difficult as originally thought.

On a videotape produced by the partnership, Lambert Dolphin, the group's geophysicist, says he has identified a large cavern under the northwest side of the peak and it may be accessible by digging a modest tunnel into the peak. He theorizes there may have been an opening down on the side of the peak long ago which allowed people hiding the treasure to simply walk into the room.

In May Dolphin used a new ground penetrating radar to make images of the peak's interior. He says the radar is 20 times more powerful than the one used in 1977 when he tested the mountain during Operation Goldfinder. After hundreds of readings from different angles, he says he has a definite picture of the room and it turns out to be 200 feet below the old Gaddis tunnel which was completed in 1963.

He says this makes sense because the family has always claimed Doc went down, by his own estimate, 300 to 400 feet into the peak. The Gaddis tunnel is 200 feet below the chimney opening on top of the peak.

Dolphin says this puts the room under the bioherm limestone reef material in the peak. A bioherm is a mass of limestone formed by organisms. He says the layer below the reef is soft shale which has probably eroded out leaving a room with crumbling walls and a very hard ceiling. He feels Noss could have entered the peak on top, worked his way to the diorite dike and its fissure and followed it down to the room.

On the tape Dolphin concludes all this is good news for the partnership and its backers. First of all, he has proof there is a cavern of some sort. Second, its location should eliminate the need for long and costly tunnels. Third, he says, "I doubt that anybody has been in that cavern since Doc Noss was there."

He goes on to assure backers that most of the gold is still there by saying, "If any artifacts or gold have been removed in recent years, these are probably secondary deposits and I would suspect not the main deposit."

Not only is this good news for hopeful backers it seems to say the Army really didn't steal the gold as "Unsolved Mysteries" and others have accused.

The tape's narrator then asks if all this work is worth it. He goes on to say that Doc Noss reported seeing more than 16,000 bars of gold in the cavern. This is total gross weight of 640,000 pounds (works out to be 40 lbs. per bar) which turns out to be 384,000 pounds of gold if each bar is only 60 percent gold. He then multiples that out at $350 per ounce and gets a value of $2,150,000,000. That's right, more than two billion dollars. Enough said.

In addition to letting the Army off the hook for stealing the gold, the tape admits the Gaddis Mining Company work at Victorio Peak in 1963 was done under contract to Ova Noss as well as the state of New Mexico. In the past many Noss supporters have said Ova was never allowed into the missile range to search for her "personal property." Now the partnership admits she was allowed in and says she was not allowed "adequate time" to recover her property---Gaddis Mining was on site 60 days in the 1963 search.

Another interesting aspect of the tape is its tone. Most of the time it is fairly straight forward. But when discussing the history of their project, the narrator makes it sound as if the Army demanded the partnership get Congress to approve the venture. The narrator states they got the Congressional support and it is now law that the partnership is authorized to dig at Victorio Peak.

In reality, the partnership was told by the Army it could not dig unless it could directly reimburse the Army for required support. It turns out this requires Congressional intervention and they were directed to seek the necessary action on the Hill. If the Army was not concerned about reimbursement, it would not require an act of Congress to approve the permit.

The rider on the 1990 Appropriations Bill says, "The Secretary of the Army may, subject to such terms and conditions as the Secretary considers appropriate to protect the interests of the United States, issue a revocable license to the Ova Noss Family Partnership...." The operative words in that sentence are "may" and "revocable." The secretary is certainly not directed to allow the search.

The key to the section follows and states that, "The Secretary of the Army shall require the Ova Noss Family Partnership to reimburse the Department of Army...." and that "Reimbursements for such costs shall be credited to the Department of the Army appropriation from which the costs were paid." This allows the partnership to reimburse WSMR directly for support costs.

This may sound like a fine distinction but it is important because contrary to what the partnership implies, there was no law passed which directs the Army to allow them onto WSMR. I can see that this would be an important point to the partnership and its various supporters and financial backers. If there was such a law, their position and efforts would be more secure, especially in dealing with the missile range.

As of the end of Fiscal Year 1990, White Sands has collected just over $122,000 for range support from the partnership. This includes such things as security, scheduling, helicopter support, archaeological work and photography.

As far as the actual search is concerned, it could begin soon. The range has received comments from the various state and federal agencies which are required to review the environmental assessment. The comments are being addressed by the author of the document and should be ready for final review and public comment soon.

Once the license is signed logistical work will begin in the Hembrillo Basin. For instance, the road must be improved, telephone lines laid to the peak and trailers placed for support personnel.

Whether the press will be allowed in to observe remains to be seen.

On July 20 the Ova Noss Family Partnership began its search for the celebrated treasure supposedly discovered by Doc Noss in Victorio Peak in 1937. So far, the search has failed to yield any treasure or any real clues on how to access the large chamber the partnership says is under the mountain.

The partnership did fix the road from the missile range's west boundary to Victorio Peak so they could get their equipment on the site. Unfortunately, not all their equipment is available yet.

They hope to drill bore holes into he peak as far as 400 feet down. The plan is to break into a large cavern which ground radar has reportedly detected. Then they will lower a specially designed probe into the hole. The probe is equipped with lights, a small video camera which feeds live signals to the surface, a range-finder and digital compass. If they are lucky they will confirm the existence of the room and possibly find an easy access to it. If they are really lucky, they will turn on the camera and see a stack of gold bars.

The drilling rig for this operation has been unavailable and may not be until later this month. In the meantime, the partnership expanded their original request and asked for permission to do a metal detector sweep of the area. There intent was to try to find some of the gold bars that Doc Noss supposedly buried the night before he was killed in March 1949.

Tony Jolley visited the site the first day to give the searchers an idea of where to run their metal detectors. Jolley says he helped Noss bury about 100 bars that night. The newspapers have reported that Jolley came back years later and dug up 10 of the golden bars and sold them for $65,000. He indicated they should concentrate on the ridges and flat areas northwest and northeast of Victorio Peak.

Because the area the group searched is right in the middle of the U.S. Cavalry Victorio battle site, all work was observed by an archaeologist representing the Army. Any time they got an indication of a metal object, the spot was marked. Most of the things they found are related to the battle and includes things like rifle cartridges. Later, the missile range may be able to use these locations to help recreate the battle.

If they felt the item might be larger, like a gold bar, it was exposed. No gold bars were found but an anvil was discovered. Also, many shallow holes were found, which led partnership workers to speculate that trespassers, years ago, may have already searched the area.

On July 28, the partnership and the missile range conducted a press briefing at the range's Countdown Rec Center. Terry Delonas, the general partner for the partnership, briefed on the history of the treasure and what they are doing now. Slides showing computer graphics of the peak and the various cavern and tunnel locations were presented. The $100,000 down hole probe was on display and family members were on hand to talk about their experiences.

Press representatives from the Associated Press, all three television networks and all the local newspapers attended.

Also, during the second week of the search the partnership attempted to open Oren's tunnel. This opening and tunnel were discovered in the 1950s by Oren Swearingen who made regular visits to the peak when he was stationed at White Sands as a dentist.

The partnership is interested in this particular tunnel because it supposedly has a shaft at its end which Swearingen says has been hand-filled with rocks. The ground radar and computer mapping the group has done since 1990 indicates the shaft leads directly down to the large cavern and supposed treasure room in the peak. They want to look at the shaft and confirm Swearingen's ideas.

In an attempt to relocate the entrance, workers drilled several bore holes into the tunnel's estimated locale. They did not have the heavy equipment they needed for the deep holes but they were able to find a lighter unit which could easily sink a 40-foot hole. They say they encountered a void with the appropriate measurements to match the description of Oren's tunnel.

Originally, they were going to lower the special probe into one of these holes. This would have enabled them to point the camera in the direction the tunnel runs and take a compass bearing. Then they could have drawn a line down the peak to the approximate site of the now covered entrance. Unfortunately, the hole had a bend in it and the probe, which is almost four feet long, could not flex to make the turn.

On July 31, searchers reportedly found what could possibly be a new opening into the peak. Late in the day, Mike Macy and Reed Hester found a small hole and thought he felt air coming out of it. He called others over and they uncovered a few inches of hole and claim there is cool air venting out of it. They plan to investigate and see if it might be their long-sought shortcut into the peak.

EMPEROR MAXIMILIAN'S TREASURE

According to a lot of legends of the southwest, at a place called Castle Gap, about 15 miles east of Horsehead Crossing, the gold and other treasure of Emperor Maximilian may be buried. In late 1866, Maximilian saw the handwriting on the wall and decided to smuggle his treasure out of the country. He planned to take a ship along to New York along with his Empress Carlotta. He planned to have his treasure horde meet him in the United States.

A 15-wagon caravan loaded with all of the treasure that the Emperor of Mexico had amassed, to include Carlotta's Crown, was sent north under the command of several loyal retainers. Upon reaching the border, the commander of the escort decided he needed to add some additional guards and hired a group of former Confederate soldiers.

One of these new guards happened to get a look at what was in one of the wagons and a plan to take over the caravan was quickly prepared. At a signal, all of the original guards were killed and the ex-Confederate soldiers took control of Maximilian's treasure. Except for some items easily converted to cash, the treasure was buried and the wagons burned over the burial site.

According to legend, Doc Noss, found this treasure and moved it to the cavern he allegedly found on what is now White Sands Missile Range. According to information found on the internet, the Emperor's Treasure, including "Carlota's Crown", Maximilian's Empress, was found and stashed by Doc Noss, in and among 7 different caverns approximately 160 feet beneath White Sands. Also stored in these caverns is some 200+ years of other gold plunder Indians collected starting in 1680 with the Pueblo revolt. Unfortunately, the only known entrance to Victorio Peak was resealed by Doc in a mishap trying to widen the very narrow vertical entrance.

According to legend, Carlota's Crown, was indeed found by Doc Noss and photographed by his wife. This priceless crown described as being made of gold, with over 250 large diamonds and a very large Ruby. His wife said that just shortly before Doc died, he placed the crown in a sturdy half sized footlocker along with some other goodies...a quart jar half filled with uncut Rubies, 24 resmelted pure gold bars, about 80k in 1930's $100.00 Gold Certificates, Gold and Jeweled Religious items, and most importantly, four maps of other Aztec treasure locations he had discovered.

A DESCRIPTION OF THE CAVERN FOUND BY DOC NOSS[164]

According to information written by David Chandler, "In 1937 a half-Indian podiatrist named Doc Noss discovered a cache of Apache gold on what is now the White Sands Missile Range ... Much of the treasure was in the form of hundreds of stacked gold bars, plus other artifacts, such as swords, goblets, crowns, statues and other things ... Doc Noss was shot and killed by his partner Charlie Ryan in March of 1949 ... Noss was known to have taken at least 88 bars of gold out of the hidden tunnels inside the mountain." (Pages 309-310).

Childress went on to say that because of an article published in the *November, 1968* issue of *True Treasure* magazine there was renewed interest in the fabulous treasure, and a prospector named Harvey Snow was approached by three ranchers who lived in the area west of the Victorio Peak site. Snow had spent 25 years exploring the entire White Sands area, and the ranchers felt that Snow could lead them into the treasure area, bypassing the Army patrols that guarded the missile range."

Because of a story told Snow many years before by a cowboy who had followed Doc Noss to a hidden tunnel, he believed that the treasure was not at Victorio Peak, but on another peak, Hard Scrabble Peak which was also on government property.

Snow's went on to say that on the second day I found the cave with the sloping steps. I went down the steps; down and down. I don't know how far. I estimated maybe thirteen hundred or fourteen hundred steps. The bottom step, the last one was rounded at the bottom so that when you stepped on it, it would roll. It was tied to a bow and arrow with rawhide, but the rawhide had rotted a long time ago. I got in there." (Page 310).

At the bottom of the steps Snow described a big room with a stream of hot water running through it. Snow followed the tunnel from room to room; sometimes the tunnel would become so narrow that he had to get down on his hands and knees. In one room Snow Reported "I found some things. I found small stacks ... one of gold, one of copper and one of silver."

""I figured I would come back for that and went on. I next came to a big room. Here there were a bunch of side tunnels running north and south. They were all natural, nothing man made. Here where they intersected, they made a big W. I did not go down these tunnels, I stayed with the stream going west ... At the far end of the main room I found some things I cannot tell you about..."" (Page 311).

Snow's story is fascinating and virtually unbelievable to most people. He walked 14 miles in an underground tunnel. The 1400 steps or so that he walked down to the subterranean river must have been a good 800 or 900 feet below the entrance. The tunnel was crossed at least in one spot by another tunnel running at a right angle to the one he was following." (Pages 113-114).

---

[164] Chandler, David, 100 Tons of Gold.

So if this story is to be believed, there exists under the White Sands New Mexico area an extensive system of lengthy tunnels that have been there for ages. If the government wanted underground bases they would make use of these existing tunnels, yet modern researchers never seem to even hint of their existence. Why not?

According to Mr. Childress; the gold that was at one time stored in Victorio Peak has been seized by the U.S. government, particularly the Army and the CIA." And I thought the CIA was concerned with foreign intelligence. Where's the connection? The Inner Beings perhaps?

"The Army was known to have bulldozed the peak out, and even place a steel door over the entrance to the mountain ... The Army assured the state that there was no gold in Victorio Peak and never has been."

"Never-the-less Chandler shows that a top secret operation took place at White Sands Missile Range on August 10, 1961. On this date the Secret Service, with the help of certain Army personnel at the range recovered the gold, and moved it to various locations for various purposes."

These claims are backed up by, of all people, Former White House counsel, *John Dean* in his book *Blind Ambition* (1976). In it he told of CIA operations dealing with bars of gold. "Egil Krogh had described to me how, when he was bored with his deskwork, he had carried bars of gold bullion through Asia's 'Golden Triangle' in CIA planes and bargained with drug chieftains ... The gold bars used in these illegal, clandestine operations allegedly came from the tunnel system inside of Victorio Peak." (Pages 314-315).

Besides furnishing our corrupt government with the finances to destroy a generation of Americans with dangerous drugs, the bastards had a large tunnel system in place. It stands to reason that this is one of the systems they are using for their nefarious and black deeds. When will the American people wake up to the fact that there are a lot of horrible things going on ... right below our feet?

ANOTHER REFERENCE ABOUT THE TREASURE OF VICTORIO PEAK

New Mexico is a complex tapestry of natural beauty with mountains the dominant feature in the landscape. Except for the eastern fringe, no part of the state is without them. Some maps name seventy-three ranges, from Animas to Zuni. They include seven peaks rising above 13,000 feet, eighty-five more than two miles high, and more than three hundred notable enough to warrant names. All are part of the Southern Rockies, and all have their own strange tales of legends and myths. No legend, however, is more mysterious than the one associated with Victorio Peak.

Victorio Peak is a nondescript, craggy outcropping of rock barely five hundred feet tall. It is nestled near the center of a dry desert lake known as the Hembrillo Basin in the desolate wastelands of northern Dona Ana County in the southern part of the state. The Basin is a lonesome, empty place with miles and miles of solitude broken neither by fence post nor telephone wires. The nearest settlements are forty miles distant, and getting to the rugged sentinel in the forbidding Basin requires skill and dexterity in traversing the barren landscape.

The Hembrillo Basin itself is the southern gateway to the vast hundred mile stretch of blistering, arid desert known as the Jornada del Muerto. It is Spanish for "Journey of Death," and it is just that. Back in the days of early Spanish exploration, travelers would sometimes leave the lush Rio Grande Valley about fifteen miles north of Las Cruces at a place where the river cut west. Trying to continue their journey north across the barren wasteland toward Socorro usually turned into a big mistake. This route did shorten their trip by several days, but it also took the travelers into the domain of hostile Apache Indians. Many died in the Indian attacks, and many more in the unforgiving desert. It seems ironic that this bleak, forbidding wasteland would hold one of the most baffling mysteries of all time.

If ever anyone was destined to find a fortune in hidden gold, that person was Milton Ernest "Doc" Noss. He was born in Oklahoma, and he claimed that it was the Cheyenne half of him which led him on the fringe of excitement all his life. He loved the unknown, and took any variety of jobs all over the Southwest. Routine things bored him, and he never stayed too long in any one place. If adventure called, Doc was the first one on the trail.

On one of his frequent trips through southern New Mexico, he met a pretty brown-haired woman named Ova Beckworth. She was loving and generous and absolutely enamored with Doc. In 1933, Doc married Ova, whom he affectionately nicknamed "Babe." They settled down in Hot Springs, which now goes under the name of Truth or Consequences in honor of a popular television game show of the 1950's. It was here that Doc opened a foot clinic. If he was any kind of medical doctor, the records have not been found to prove it. Hot Springs was known as one of the Southwest's best health resorts. People from all over the country came to ease their aches and pains in the healing, warm water, soak up the warm sunshine, and bask in the warm New Mexico hospitality. It was not long before Babe and Doc made many friends.

In November 1937, Doc, Babe, and four others left on a deer hunt into the Hembrillo Basin. They drove toward Victorio Peak, setting up camp on the desert floor not far from the base of the peak. Early the next morning, the men headed into the wilderness, leaving the women in camp. Doc was a loner, and not wanting to hunt with so many others around, he headed toward Victorio Peak to hunt by himself.

As Doc scouted around the base of the mountain, it began to drizzle. It was only a light rain, but a cold rain, and he decided to seek shelter. Since Victorio Peak is a barren, treeless pinnacle of rock and dirt, he scampered up the peak, searching for a rocky overhang large enough to scoot under. Near the summit, he spied a huge boulder and headed toward it. He saw evidence of early inhabitants, but did not know if they had lived there long, or merely used it as a temporary shelter the way he was doing. In the dim light, while waiting for the rain to subside, he noticed a stone that looked as if it had been worked in some fashion. He reached down, but was unable to budge it. Carefully digging around it, he was finally able to work his hands under it. When he lifted it clear, he found a hole which appeared to lead straight down into the heart of the mountain.

Instantly intrigued, Doc ignored the rain and peered over the side into the gaping blackness. He saw what he took to be an old, man-made shaft with a thick, wooden pole attached at one side. The pole had deep gouges at regular intervals for footholds and appeared rotten, leading Doc to believe the opening was the entrance to an ancient, abandoned mine shaft. He totally forgot all about hunting, as he carefully positioned himself under the boulder out of the rain. He planned adventure of a different sort.

When it stopped raining, Doc returned to camp and told Babe of his discovery, cautioning her not to tell the others. It was his plan to return later and investigate the shaft privately. If it was an abandoned mine, it would not matter, but if he found gold, he did not want to share it with anyone.

Several days later, Doc and Babe Noss returned to Victorio Peak with ropes and flashlights. When Doc inched his way down through the tight, narrow passage into the mountain, he uncovered the most controversial subject in New Mexico history---a topic involving unimaginable wealth, murder and mystery. The participants are as varied as they are unique. They appear to range from Don Juan de Onate's brutal conquest of New Mexico in the 16th Century to our federal government of today, encompassing 18th Century Mexican friars and a legendary 19th Century Apache war chief along the way. It is one of the most incredible chapters in American history.

According to reports, Doc's initial journey down the shaft was nothing less than spectacular. After testing the wooden pole attached at one side and deciding it was too risky for his weight, he descended by rope nearly sixty feet through the narrow opening. Near the bottom he encountered a huge boulder hanging from the ceiling, almost blocking his way. Unknown to him at the time, this boulder would later play an important role in his adventure.

At the bottom of the narrow shaft was a chamber about the size of a small room with drawings around the walls. Doc thought these sketches were made by Indians, as they were crude and stick-like. Some were painted, while others were chiseled into the rock face. At the other end of the chamber, the shaft continued sloping downward. Descending another hundred and twenty feet before it leveled off, Doc found that the passageway emptied into a huge, natural cavern large enough "for a freight train to pass through." He saw several smaller rooms chiseled from the rock along one wall.

As Doc inched his way across the great cavern, he made a terrifying discovery...a human skeleton. The hands were bound behind the back, and the skeleton was kneeling, securely tied to a stake driven into the ground, as if the person had been deliberately left there to die. Before leaving the room, he found more skeletons, most of them bound and secured to stakes like the first. Some skeletons were found stacked in a small enclosure, as if in a burial chamber. All told, he reportedly found twenty-seven human skeletons in the caverns of the mountain.

As Doc explored the side caverns of Victorio Peak, he found amazing riches amounting to extreme wealth by today's standards. Jewels, coins, saddles, and priceless artifacts were everywhere, including a gold statue of the Virgin Mary. In one chamber, he found an old Wells Fargo box and leather pouches neatly stacked to the ceiling. He even found some old letters, the most recent of which was dated 1880. On the lid of one old chest were words written in old English script. The contents of the caverns appeared to represent several different nationalities, and it baffled him.

These chests and artifacts were only the tip of the iceberg. In a deeper cavern, Doc found what he thought was a stack of worthless pig-iron bars. He estimated there were over sixteen thousand bars weighing over forty pounds apiece "stacked up against the wall like cordwood." He was barely able to lift one, much less think of carrying it back to the surface. Later, the wealth in the cave was calculated to be worth more than two billion dollars. No matter what the estimate, it was clear that Doc had found a substantial treasure, much of it in gold bullion.

Doc filled his pockets with gold coins, grabbed a couple of jeweled swords, and laboriously returned to Babe waiting anxiously at the surface. After telling her of what he had seen and showing her the loot, she insisted he go back into the mine for one of the pig-iron bars. After much searching, he finally found a small iron bar that he could carry back through the narrow passageway, but it was difficult maneuvering through the tight passage with the heavy bar. When he reached the surface, he told Babe, "This is the last one of them babies I'm gonna bring out."

By then, it was late afternoon, the sun almost on the horizon. When Babe rolled the bar over, she noticed a yellow gleam where the gravel of the hillside had scratched off centuries of black grime. She showed the gold metal to Doc. He said, "Well Babe, if it's gold, and all that other is gold like it, we can call John D. Rockefeller a tramp."

From the time Doc Noss discovered the treasure in Victorio Peak, he and Babe spent every free moment exploring the tunnels that led deep inside the mountain. They began living in a tent at the base of the peak, working the claim each day for hours on end. On each trip, Doc would retrieve two gold bars and artifacts. At one time, he brought out a crown that Babe cleaned in her sink in town. According to Babe's report, it contained two hundred forty-three diamonds and one pigeon-blood ruby. Yet, Doc trusted no one, not even his wife. He disappeared at night into the desert with his booty, hiding pieces of the treasure in places that he never revealed.

Among the artifacts Doc is reported to have retrieved from the cache were four codices---leather pages with hand-tooled instructions---one dated 1797. According to Doc, the codices were reburied in the desert in a chest with other artifacts. Although the originals have never been recovered, there was a copy of one, a translation of which explains the significance of the number seven, according to Pope Pius III.

"Seven is the holy number," the passage begins. It then continues for several lines before ending with a cryptic message: "In seven languages, seven signs, and languages in seven foreign nations, look for the Seven Cities of Gold. Seventy miles north of El Paso del Norte in the seventh peak, Soledad, these cities have seven sealed doors, three sealed toward the rising of the Sol sun, three sealed toward the setting of the Sol sun, one deep within Casa del Cueva de Oro, at high noon. Receive health, wealth, and honor."

Believers say that Doc Noss found the Casa del Cueva de Oro, Spanish for the House of the Golden Cave. "Soledad" was the former name of Victorio Peak, and Doc apparently found the seventh door located "at high noon," but the promised health, wealth, and honor were denied him. Four years before his discovery, Congress had passed the Gold Act, which outlawed the private ownership of gold. Doc was unable to profit from his treasure on the open market.

When Doc's story eventually hit the headlines, scholars began speculating on how the enormous treasure could have come to be stashed inside Victorio Peak. It was not hard to come up with theories. New Mexico has undergone a lot of transition from the time of the earliest friars to modern time. One of the theories scholars advanced dates back to Don Juan de Onate, who, in 1598, founded New Mexico as a Spanish colony. He knew the tales of the Seven Cities of Gold, and he surely sought them. But Onate was cruel, brutally subjugating the Indians to do his bidding. He beat and tortured them, forcing them to mine gold and silver. It has been reported that he amassed a treasure of gold, silver and jewels before being ordered to Mexico City in 1607. If he did not take the fortune with him, he must have stored it somewhere...Victorio Peak perhaps?

Another theory is that the treasure belonged to a Catholic missionary named Felipe La Rue, or La Ruz, as church documents are said to give his name. He was a native of France and was among the small group of priests who volunteered for service in Mexico. His party sailed to Florida, crossed the Gulf of Mexico to Vera Cruz, and from there, it went to Mexico City by ox cart. After a short rest, Padre La Rue left for the north, where he took up his work among the Indians and peons at a large hacienda near what is now the city of Chihuahua, reaching there in 1798.

From the people at his new station, he heard stories about a fabulous source of rich minerals in the mountains to the north. If he was interested in these stories, he did not reveal it to others. Instead, he continued with his teachings and ministering to the sick and spiritual needs of his small parish. Among his parishioners was an old man, who had been an explorer and soldier of fortune during his youth. This man had traveled widely over the country to the north, and as Padre La Rue personally cared for this ailing old man, the two became good friends.

One day, Padre La Rue asked about the riches which lay to the north. The old man said that if the good priest wanted gold, there was a rich deposit of it located high in the mountains about two days' travel north of El Paso del Norte, which is the present-day site of El Paso, Texas. According to the legend, the man said, "After one day's travel from El Paso del Norte, you will come to three small peaks yet further to the north. Upon first sight of these peaks, turn to the east and cross the desert toward the mountains. In the mountains, you will find a basin where there is a spring at the foot of a solitary peak. On this peak, you will find gold." A few days later, the old man died.

It was not until the crops failed that Padre La Rue thought of the solitary peak filled with gold. His little parish needed water and a better climate, and he called everyone together, asking if they would follow him north. They all agreed, and the little party set out for their new country. After crossing El Paso del Norte, they followed the course of the Rio Grande to the small village of La Mesilla near Las Cruces. North of there, they sighted the three peaks and turned east across the dreaded Jornada del Muerto, finally arriving in the San Andreas Mountains. After a couple of days of exploration, they located a basin in which there was a spring at the base of a solitary peak, just as the old man had said.

Scholars all believe this basin was the Hembrillo Basin, and the solitary peak was Soledad Peak. After a fierce battle between the Army and Chief Victorio of the Apaches in 1880, the peak assumed a new name of Victorio Peak. It is not to be confused with Victoria Peak in the Black Range Mountains near Kingston, New Mexico.

Padre La Rue established a crude camp and sent the men out to search for the gold the old man had promised was there. On one side of the peak, they located a rich vein, ultimately working the mine for years. They tunneled into the mountain and followed the vein downward. The deeper they went, the richer the ore became. The little priest assigned dozens of monks and Indians to mine the gold, form it into ingots and, except for whatever was needed for supplies, stack it along one wall of a natural cavern inside the mountain.

Word eventually reached church officials in Mexico City that the hacienda had been abandoned, and Padre La Rue's tiny colony was missing. A search party went to investigate. When they returned and reported that the entire population had left for the mountains to the north, soldiers were dispatched with orders to locate the priest and demand an explanation.

It was when a small group was in La Mesilla purchasing supplies that they learned the Mexican Army was on the horizon. Hurrying to camp, they spread the alarm. It was one thing for Padre La Rue to leave his post without permission of church officials in Mexico City, but it was quite another not to deliver the Royal Fifth (or Quinta) of the gold for shipment to Spain. Padre La Rue was in a lot of trouble.

Padre La Rue immediately set about concealing all traces of the mine. Working day and night, knowing the soldiers were drawing ever closer, he had his little group labor to conceal the entrance. When the soldiers finally arrived and demanded to know where the gold came from which was used to purchase the supplies in La Mesilla, Padre La Rue refused to answer. He died under torture, as did many of his followers, and although the soldiers looked all over for evidence of a mine, they were forced to return to Mexico City with nothing to show for their long journey. The Lost Padre Mine, as it has been called ever since, went into the history pages as a beloved legend.

Many scholars think that Doc Noss stumbled upon the Lost Padre Mine, but there are a few who speculate that the treasure could be the missing wealth of Emperor Maxmilian. As emperor of Mexico in the 1860's, Maxmilian attempted to get his gold out of Mexico, especially when he learned of an assassination plot. He was, in fact, assassinated in 1867. Legend says he sent a palace full of valuables to the United States, and it has never been found. Although it has been rumored that it went by ship and lies in deep waters off the coast of New Orleans, the victim of a particularly bad Gulf storm, the easiest route for the Maxmilian treasure train would have been through the New Mexico corridor into Texas. Strangely, there is an old rumor that it has been lost along the dunes of shifting lake bed in West Texas, the victim of banditry where all the bandits were killed by pursuing posse members. The truth is that no one knows anything for certain. Could the jewels and coins Doc saw have been part of Maxmilian's missing fortune?

And how does Chief Victorio enter into the story? Well, the most colorful legend associated with the Victorio Peak treasure does concern the great Warm Springs Apache war chief. Victorio used the entire Hembrillo Basin as his stronghold. He absolutely refused to live on the San Carlos Reservation in Arizona where his people died from hunger and insect bites. Victorio's land had always been in the mountains of New Mexico, and a treaty between the Federal government in Washington and his band had promised they could stay on those lands as long as the "mountains stand and the rivers flowed." With the discovery of gold in the mountains, such did not happen, and in 1878, the treaty was broken. Victorio went on the war path. Knowing how much the white man valued gold and having little use for it himself, he amassed huge amounts of the yellow mineral any way he could get it. He and his warriors raided throughout the Jornada and the Rio Grande Valley, attacking wagon trains, churches, immigrants, mail coaches, and anything else that promised riches. He raided the stage lines all over southern New Mexico and Texas in an all-out war against the U. S. Army and the Texas Rangers. He also took prisoners back to the Basin and subjected them to elaborate torture as a test of their bravery before killing them. Were the skeletons found inside Victorio Peak victims of Victorio's raids?

On 7 April 1880, Victorio engaged in a fierce battle with a troop of the 9th Cavalry Buffalo Soldiers at the mountain. After a bloody standoff that resulted in the deaths of many of the soldiers, the Army retreated. The peak was thereafter known as Victorio Peak in honor of the great chief. Many researchers believe that Victorio and his Apaches had an entrance into the mountain and that they used the cave to conceal the booty they looted from the surrounding areas. It would also explain the presence of the Wells Fargo bags, the pack saddles, the letters and other artifacts dating to Victorio's time. Did the Apaches fight hard to protect their cache of treasures within the mountain?

It is doubtful Doc Noss cared anything about the historical value of the fortune inside the hollow peak. The pouches and packs, artifacts and leather goods were mostly ignored, while he concentrated on the gold coins and bars. Ever since he found the treasure, he worked stealthily to remove what he could of it. He never told any of friends what he was doing.

Finally, in the spring of 1938, Doc Noss and Babe went to Santa Fe to establish legal ownership of his find. He filed a lease with the State of New Mexico for the entire section of land surrounding Victorio Peak. Subsequent to that, he filed mining claims on and around Victorio Peak. He had it surveyed for an exact location, and then filed a treasure trove claim, which has become the historic Noss family claim to the treasure in Victorio Peak. With legal ownership established, he worked his claim openly, but he became super cautious. He took the gold bars out of the cavern and then hid them from everyone, including his own family, in a variety of locations all over the desert. Some were right by the county roads by certain marked telephone poles. Some were dropped in horse tanks at the nearby ranches. Some were just buried in the sand, and Doc would put a different colored rock over the top than was natural to that surrounding.

There was a lot of fear and probably some increasing paranoia in both Doc and Babe. As they solicited more and more help from friends, neighbors, and supporters, they became afraid that some of these people might try to steal some of the bullion that they had hidden around the Peak.

It was the Fall of 1939 when Doc made his great mistake. He decided to enlarge the passageway into Victorio Peak, reasoning that if he could rid the narrow quarters of the confining huge boulder hanging at the lower portion of the shaft, he could removed the gold much easier and, more importantly, much faster. He hired a mining engineer named S.E. Montgomery to go with him and help him blast out the shaft. Although Doc claimed the mountain was rotten, and the two men argued viciously about the charge to used, Montgomery won the argument. The choice was eight sticks of dynamite.

The blast was disastrous. Instead of widening the passage as Doc wanted, it caused a cave-in, collapsing the fragile shaft and effectively shutting Doc out of his own mine. Doc tried several times to regain entry into his mine, but the shaft was sealed with tons of debris. All attempts failed, leaving him embittered and angry. He took to taking his frustrations out on his wife, and it was not long before Babe and Doc divorced. Now, instead of having thousands of gold bars to draw from, he only had those few hundred that he had brought to the surface. He became very protective of those gold bars. Two years after his divorce from Babe, he married Violet Lena Boles, which would further complicate ownership of the treasure rights in the years to come.

When Doc became desperate for cash, he took into his confidence a man named Joseph Andregg. The two of them transported gold bars, coins, jewels, and artifacts into Arizona, selling them on the black market. For nine years, Doc attempted illegally to sell his gold, but it was difficult finding buyers. He was afraid of getting caught and ending up in prison. His paranoia increased daily.

In 1949, Doc met a miner named Charley Ryan from Alice, Texas. He became convinced that Ryan could reopen the shaft, and he arranged to exchange some of the gold bars for $25,000 to fund the venture. Meanwhile, Babe Noss had filed a counter-claim on the entire area. Denied entry by the courts until legalities could determine the legal owner of the mine, Doc feared Ryan would back out of the deal. Sensing a double-cross and that Ryan would abscond with fifty-one bars of re-hidden gold, Doc asked an acquaintance, Tony Jolly, to help him rebury the gold in a new hiding place. The trip made a believer out of Jolly.

"We got in the pickup, and we went out across the desert a long ways," said Jolly, "and we started digging. We dug twenty bars of gold out of the ground right there. I said, 'Doc, what's going on?' and he said, 'Well, there's a fella coming tomorrow who's gonna fly in here, and he's supposed to take this gold and sell it, and he's supposed to split with me. I got word that he's gonna sell it and keep right on going with the money.' We reburied those bars of gold. There turned out to be ninety more. I handled, and I saw one hundred and ten bars of gold."

The next day Doc and Ryan got into an argument, and Ryan pulled a gun on Doc. Ryan insisted that they discuss the problem of what happened to the gold that Doc had re-hidden, hinting that if Doc did not reveal its new hiding place, Doc would not live to enjoy the gold. A fight ensued. As Doc Noss headed toward his car, Ryan, fearing Doc was getting a gun, shot in Doc's direction. The bullet struck Doc in the head, killing him instantly. The date was 5 March 1949. Just twelve years after discovering the treasure, Doc Noss died kneeling in the dust with only $2.16 in his pocket. Ryan was charged with murder, but was later acquitted.

As the years passed, Babe Noss held onto her claim at Victorio Peak, occasionally hiring men to help her clear the shaft. Things were plodding along until 1955, when White Sands Missile Range unexpectedly expanded their operations to encompass the Hembrillo Basin. The military locked Babe out. Although Babe corresponded regularly with the military requesting permission to enter the range and work her claim, she was always denied. The military was afraid that allowing her permission would set a precedent that would allow others to petition and make similar claims. It would hinder the Army's mission, which was missile testing. From that moment onward, every attempt of Babe's to clear the rubble from the plugged shaft met with a military escort out of the area.

The real problem with the military claim on the land stemmed from a statement made by state officials in New Mexico. On 14 November 1951, Public Land Order No. 703 was issued, which withdrew all the White Sands Proving Ground (later to be called the White Sands Missile Range) from prospecting, entry, location, and purchase under the mining laws and reserved their use for the military. But the state officials claimed that they leased only the surface of the land to the military. The underground wealth, in whatever form it took, still belonged to the state, or to the holders of the various types of licenses. If there was treasure on the land, it did not belong to the Army, but it might not have belonged to Doc Noss, either. A search of mining records in December 1950 failed to turn up any existing mining claims, which Doc claimed he had filed. Further, Roy Henderson owned the land where Victorio Peak is located, and he had leased it to the Army. Before him, the Gilmore family had lived there. In other words, much of the disputed land belonged not to the Noss family, but to someone else.

Babe Noss then contacted the two senators from New Mexico, hoping to enlist their help in mining her claim. In December 1952, Senator Dennis Chavez wrote to Brigadier General G. G. Eddy about the problem on the White Sands Proving Grounds. Senator Clinton P. Anderson also wrote to General Eddy, but the general ruled that no further operations would be allowed on the peak because the paperwork was already being prepared to transfer all mineral rights to the government. The dispute was finally worked out in federal court which settled on a compromise of sorts. The Army would continue to use the surface of the land, but no one would be allowed on the Proving Grounds without the Army's consent. In effect, no one could mine the treasure, and that included the Army and Babe Noss, but that did not deter Babe. She refused to leave, claiming that all she wanted, according to all the letters and documents she sent, was to recover what her late husband had discovered.

By 1958, few people believed in Babe's claim of hidden gold. Doc was dead, and with his death went the location of all the buried bars of bullion he had removed from the peak before sealing himself out of the mountain. With the passage of years, few people could claim to have seen any of the treasure. Even though the military always refused any of Babe's efforts to work her claim, it apparently did not refuse other military personnel from exploring portions of the White Sands. The fat hit the fire when two airmen from nearby Holloman Air Force Base said they had penetrated the gold cavern from another natural opening in the side of Victorio Peak.

The soldiers, Airman First Class Thomas Berlett and Captain Leonard V. Fiege, said they had penetrated a fissure which led to a small cavern filled with approximately one hundred gold bars weighing between forty and eighty pounds each. The bars were shaped like house bricks. Neither man was familiar with laws governing the discovery of treasure on a military reservations, nor were they aware that the Whites Sands command did not hold the mineral rights to anything found on the Range. Fiege told several people that he had caved in the roof and walls to make it look as if the tunnel came to a dead end, and then both men covered the entrance with rocks and dirt to disguise the location. Fiege then went to the Judge Advocate's Office at Holloman Air Force Base and conferred with Colonel Sigmund I. Gasiewicz.

There was now two separate military commands involved. Gasiewicz called the Land Office in Santa Fe and spoke to a Land Office attorney named

Oscar Jordan, saying that an officer assigned to the command at Holloman Air Force Base had found a gold bar on White Sands Proving Grounds, an Army post. Jordan suggested the gold bar be sent to the Department of the Treasury or to the Secret Service, since Jordan was under the impression that Fiege had carried a gold bar to the JAG office at Holloman. Both Fiege and Gasiewicz denied that this happened, but they did form a corporation to protect what Fiege had found. They planned to contact the various governmental agencies to make sure they violated no laws, and they planned to make a formal application to enter White Sands for a search and retrieval of the gold. Although the military issued an edict forbidding them to go back and remove any gold, gold fever still struck. This time the gold seekers were the U. S. Army.

In the summer of 1961, Captain Fiege, Captain Orby Swanner, Major Kelly, and Colonel Gorman were instructed by Major General John Shinkle of White Sands to work the Noss claim on advice from the director of the Mint, who had been bothered by many requests for additional information on the treasure. General Shinkle did not want anyone on the installation not authorized to be there, but he was interested in solving the mystery once and for all. However, he was unwilling to set a precedent that would haunt all of them in the future, so he requested the permission from the Department of the Army to allow a search. On 5 August, Fiege and his party returned to Victorio Peak, accompanied by the commander of the Missile Range, a secret service agent, and fourteen military police. Try as he would, Captain Fiege was unable to penetrate the opening he had used just three years earlier. General Shinkle finally had enough of it and ordered everyone out. Fiege took a lie detector test, and the results of that test prompted General Shinkle to allow Fiege back on the missile range. This time, the military to began a full-scale mining operation at the Peak.

In October of that year, fueled by increasing suspicions that the military was working her claim, Babe Noss hired four men to surreptitiously enter the range. These men were caught trespassing, and after being escorted from the area, they reported to Babe that they observed several men in Army fatigues on the peak. In an affidavit dated 28 October 1961, one of the men, Judge H.L. Moreland of Loveland, Texas, claimed they saw a military jeep, a weapons carrier, a number of poles about the width of telephone poles, and other timbers which were cut and notched.

In his affidavit, Judge Moreland testified that his group talked to Captain Orby Swanner, who ordered them to leave the missile range. As soon as he could, Moreland reported the Army activity on Victorio Peak to Babe Noss. She told Oscar Jordan with the New Mexico State Land Office, and Jordan contacted the Judge Advocate's Office at White Sands Missile Range. In December 1961, General Shinkle shut down the operation and excluded all from the range who were not engaged in missile research activities

Thirty days later, under cover of darkness, Moreland and his friends returned to the Peak. It was totally deserted. Moreland saw the remains of extensive excavations, apparently carried out by the government. There were roads and scaffolds and tunnels, but as for Babe Noss' gold treasure, there was no sign of it.

The Gaddis Mining Company of Denver, Colorado, under a $100,000 contract to the Denver Mint, and working with the Museum of New Mexico in Santa Fe, obtained permission from the military to dig the site in 1963. Since it was a state sponsored research trip, designed to uncover artifacts of archaeological significance, the Army readily agreed. For three months, beginning on 20 June 1963, using a variety of techniques, they mapped the peak, searching for large void area that would indicate caverns. They removed tons of earth, dug their own tunnel into the side of the peak, but no entrance to any treasure cache occurred. They also dug a number of small test holes ranging in depth from 18 to 175 feet. When they ceased operations, they were a quarter of a million dollars poorer for their searching which failed to turn up anything.

It was during this same period that the Department of the Army asked Babe Noss to sign a consent document allowing the Army to search. What it said was that she waived all rights to sue the Army or the government "for alleged unlawful taking and withholding of her personal property." Under advise from her attorney, she was advised not to sign, but she had already signed the document when her attorney learned of it. What he wanted to know was why the Army would insist on such a waiver? Was it an indirect admission that there had been unauthorized intrusion into the cavern by military personnel?

It turns out that there are two theories to this document. First, only Doc Noss had ever been inside the peak, and it is only his word that gold bars were stacked there. Although Leonard Fiege had been inside a cavern, he had been feeling sick the day he was there, and all he saw were bricks covered in dust. They may or may not have been gold bars. There are some who think that Doc salted the cave in an attempt to defraud others. So, for the Army to have Babe sign such a waiver document, might not they be guarding against a real possibility that once the cavern was opened, nothing would be found in it? If Babe then believed that the Army or the government had beaten her into the cave and "stolen" the treasure that belonged to her, she would not be able to file suit. It would make no difference if the gold had been there or not, or even if the treasure cave was a myth or not. What mattered was that the Army would be protected from lawsuits.

In 1972, F. Lee Bailey, a nationally known attorney, became involved. He claimed to represent fifty unidentified clients "who knew the location of the cave with one hundred tons of gold stacked within." These claimants had retained Bailey to help them find a legal means to work the claim on the federal reservation. Bailey was skeptical, but was provided with one of the bars for analysis. He sent it to the Treasury for testing. It was sixty percent gold and forty percent copper. The problem is that fourteen-karat gold is about fifty-eight percent gold and forty-two percent copper. It was noted that old gold ingots were often far from pure. No real conclusion could be drawn from the tests. Also, the

Senate Watergate hearings were in progress, and the matter was not pursued through Federal channels. Again, Babe Noss was not one of the claimants.

Meanwhile, there were now all sorts of claimants in the issue. Along with Babe Noss, there was the group formed around Fiege, Violet Noss Yancy, something called the Shriver group, the Bailey claimants, and Expeditions Unlimited (a Florida based treasure hunting group). The Army, suffering a guilty conscience perhaps, finally allowed Expeditions Unlimited, representing all of the groups, including Babe Noss and Airman Thomas Berlett, to excavate the peak in 1977. Berlett reported that 'if the mountain has not been penetrated and no materials removed from the mountain, this will be the biggest thing that this country has ever seen.' However, the Army placed a two week time limit on the group, and they had hardly started before they had to quit. What was most valuable, from the Army's point of view, was that those claiming something was hidden in Victorio Peak had had their chance to search. They had found nothing. The Army then shut down all operations and said no additional searches would be allowed.

It was not the end of Babe's quest for her mine. Her story spread like tentacles across the land, becoming profiled in several magazines and newspaper articles. Although Babe died in 1979, he grandson, Terry Delonas, fully intended to continue the family tradition. He formed the Ova Noss Family Partnership. By 1989, the story of the Noss family treasure claim had reached millions of Americans. Incredibly, another piece of the Victorio Peak puzzle then surfaced.
It came from a retired couple living in Baytown near Houston, Texas. Captain Swanner was stationed at White Sands Missile Range in the early 1960's, and he apparently told member of his family about the Victorio Peak mystery. He said that he had gone to inspect and confirm that the treasure as reported by Airman Berlett and Captain Fiege did exist. He was Chief of Security at the time. When he determined the accuracy of the two men's reports, he put the entire area off-limits until an official investigation could be conducted. His superiors notified the Pentagon.

Supposedly, the military was able to penetrate at least one of the secret caves and inventory the contents, although the gold bars were supposedly removed by the Army to Fort Knox. The Pentagon confirmed that Captain Swanner had served as an officer assigned to security at White Sands Missile Range in 1961. However, Gordon Hobbs, from the Office of the Assistant Secretary of the Army, responded to the allegations reported of Captain Swanner by his relatives by saying that he really did not know anything. He had never seen any such claim in any of the records he had examined, and he had heard nothing of any such claim in the inquiries he had conducted. It did not mean it had never happened, it just meant that Gordon Hobbs could find no record of it.

For Gordon Hobbs to be telling the truth, and there is no reason for him to lie, the official records may have been altered or destroyed or there was never anything in the peak in the first place. On the other hand, what was all the covert military operation on the peak that Judge Moreland and his friends witnessed in

1961? Furthermore, the Army certainly knew of the Noss claim. Babe Noss had been in contact with them for years to gain access to it. If it could ever be proved that the Army stole Babe's treasure, would not the Army then be liable for restitution? Under that assumption, would not it be better for the Army to conveniently lose, misplace, or destroy any records that might have existed to support that accusation?

The Army's official position on the whereabouts of the gold is still a cautious one. According to Jim Eckles, civilian public affairs officer at White Sands Missile Range at the time this section was written, the burden of proof rests with the accusers. There is just no way of satisfying everyone involved in this mystery.

Some researchers believe the Army really did retrieve much of the gold and then perpetrated a cover-up. They point out that the army spent hundreds of thousands of dollars digging and excavating Victorio Peak. They also point out that the Army built roads and even placed a locked steel door over the original shaft discovered by Doc Noss. Why...if not to conceal?

Was Captain Orby Swanner telling the truth? Did the Army remove the gold from Victorio Peak? Is there any physical evidence that Captain Swanner, or anyone for that matter, was ever, in fact, inside Victorio Peak in 1961? There are some who claim that Swanner left evidence of his presence in the cave, and that during the 1977 excavation, military debris---battery packs and such---was found. There is also the claim that they photographed a name and a date and an Army serial number on the wall of one of the tunnels. The name was Capt. Orby Swanner. The date was 7 OCT 1961.

Understandably, members of the Noss family and their friends believe that the military may have exploited Babe's claim and that the treasure is now gone. They think soldiers may have moved it out by October 1961. But it is also entirely possible that the treasure still remains. The codices mentioned a total of seven entrances into the peak---presumably doorways to seven different treasure locations. Doc Noss' was the summit; Captain Fiege's was along one side. Suppose there are others?

Terry Delongas just doesn't know. "We're not accusing the military of stealing the gold, but I do feel that the Department of the Army in the 1960's treated my grandmother unfairly. They really tried to make a fool out of her, and all the time she was telling the truth. They had sent my grandmother on a wild goose chase for decades. If that is the fact, I think a great injustice has been done. However, we've worked very hard over the years to establish a working relationship with the military, and we're certainly not going to jeopardize that by accusing them of theft."

It is doubtful anyone will know the truth about Victorio Peak until it is thoroughly excavated. There is no doubt a treasure existed; it has been photographed, affidavits are on file from those who have seen it, and Babe Noss had relics from it. Researchers also believe that the mine of Father La Rue was the hiding place of Chief Victorio's plunder...and Doc Noss' discovery.

Babe Noss died in 1979 and since then, her heirs have continued to push the Army for permission to excavate the peak. A special act of Congress, House Bill 2461 passed in 1989, has unlocked the Hembrillo Basin for Terry Delonas and the other heirs of Babe Noss to investigate. The Partnership has been allowed back on the range, but as late as 1995, they had still found nothing. The search is on-going.

Is the treasure still there? No one knows for sure. With all the blasting and digging that has occurred on the peak over the past sixty years, it may be impossible to economically excavate. But if it does still exist, the entire treasure today is estimated to be worth more than $1.7 billion dollars.

So there you have it. If the old stories are to be believed, Fort Bliss and its adjacent installations may just be sitting on top of a king's ransom in gold and other valuables. But are these stories true? There is only one way to find out.

PICTURES

INDEX

**IF YOU ENJOYED THIS BOOK THEN YOU NEED TO READ
SPIRITS OF THE BORDER: THE HISTORY AND MYSTERY OF
EL PASO DEL NORTE**

ALSO
READ THE BOOK THAT PREDICTED 9/11
WRITTEN IN 1992,
THIS PROPHETIC NOVEL READS LIKE AN
AFTER ACTION REPORT OF THE TERRORIST
ATTACK ON NEW YORK CITY

ALSO AVAILABLE IS
VOLUME II OF MANHATTAN CONSPIRACY,
SUBTITLED CAPITAL CRIMES
WHERE THE CONSPIRACY CONTINUES

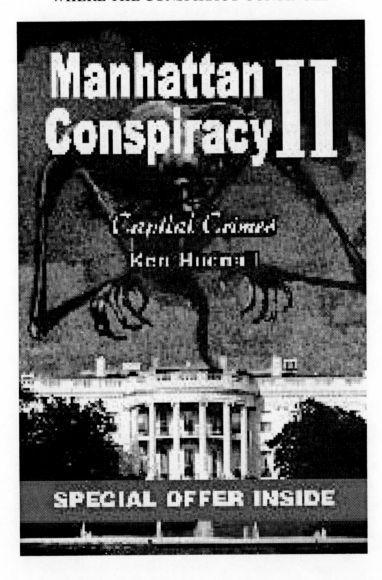

**RELEASED IN OCTOBER 2003 IS THE THIRD VOLUME IN THE
MANHATTAN CONSPIRACY SAGE ENTITLED ANGEL OF DEATH.
WILL A MAN WHOSE LIFE HAS BEEN DESTROYED BY AGENTS OF
HIS OWN COUNTRY RISK WHAT IS LEFT OF HIS LIFE TO SAVE
THAT COUNTRY?**

Printed in the United States
17192LVS00006B/160-201